Table of Contents
LEVEL B

Table of Contents
LEVEL B

Unit 7

Here's what to do!
Print the capital and small letters of the alphabet.

A a

① m ___ o

② t ___ v

③ d ___ f

④ a ___ c

⑤ p ___ r

⑥ g ___ i

⑦ r ___ t

⑧ o ___ q

⑨ s ___ u

⑩ x ___ z

⑪ j ___ l

⑫ v ___ x

Now try this! Print the letters that come before and after each letter.

① ___ k ___

② ___ w ___

③ ___ s ___

④ ___ o ___

⑤ ___ q ___

⑥ ___ d ___

⑦ ___ h ___

⑧ ___ m ___

⑨ ___ x ___

⑩ ___ c ___

⑪ ___ i ___

⑫ ___ t ___

Here's what to do! Begin at the ★. Follow the alphabet from dot to dot to make a letter in each box. Circle that capital and small letter each time you find it in the words.

①

```
a    b      e    f
★    •      •    •

     c•    •d

     j•    •i

•    •      •    •
l    k      h    g
```

Happy
hello
birthday
surprise
Here
Mother

②

```
d    e      g    h
★    •      •    •
            f
            •
     m•    •k

            •
            l
•    •      •    •
o    n      j    i
```

something
make
rain
Some
Must
Name

③

```
m    n
★    •


        •o      p
                •

•              •
r              q
```

look
Little
Hello
milk
Sally
will

④

```
p    q      s    t
★    •      •    •



     w•        •r


•    •      •    •
y    x      v    u
```

Nuts
know
children
farm
new
soon

⑤

```
s              t
★              •


•    •    •    •
z    y    v    u



     •    •
     x    w
```

Wants
letters
help
Tom
went
Time

⑥

```
u    v      x    y
★    •      •    •


            •
            w



            •
            z
```

Live
loves
Vine
every
went
ever

LESSON 2: Alphabetical order   5

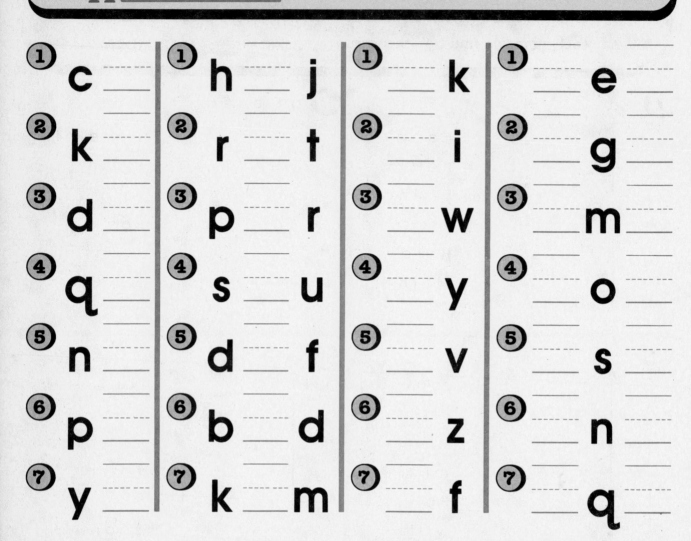

① c _____
② k _____
③ d _____
④ q _____
⑤ n _____
⑥ p _____
⑦ y _____

① h _____ j _____
② r _____ t _____
③ p _____ r _____
④ s _____ u _____
⑤ d _____ f _____
⑥ b _____ d _____
⑦ k _____ m _____

① k _____
② i _____
③ w _____
④ y _____
⑤ v _____
⑥ z _____
⑦ f _____

① _____ e _____
② _____ g _____
③ _____ m _____
④ _____ o _____
⑤ _____ s _____
⑥ _____ n _____
⑦ _____ q _____

Now try this! Print the missing letters to complete the alphabet.

a _____

_____ k _____

_____ u _____

f _____

_____ y _____

i _____

_____ q _____

Here's what to do! Say the name of each picture. Print the capital and small letters for its beginning sound.

1

2

3

4

5

6

7

8

9

10

11

12

LESSON 3: Initial consonants

7

Here's what to do!

Say the name of each picture. Print the letter for its beginning sound.

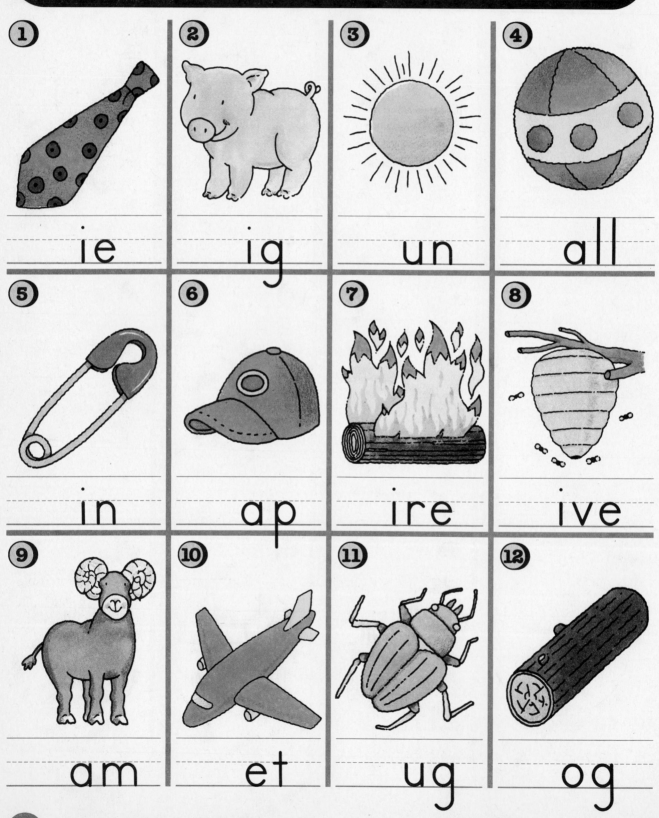

1. ___ie

2. ___ig

3. ___un

4. ___all

5. ___in

6. ___ap

7. ___ire

8. ___ive

9. ___am

10. ___et

11. ___ug

12. ___og

LESSON 3: Initial consonants

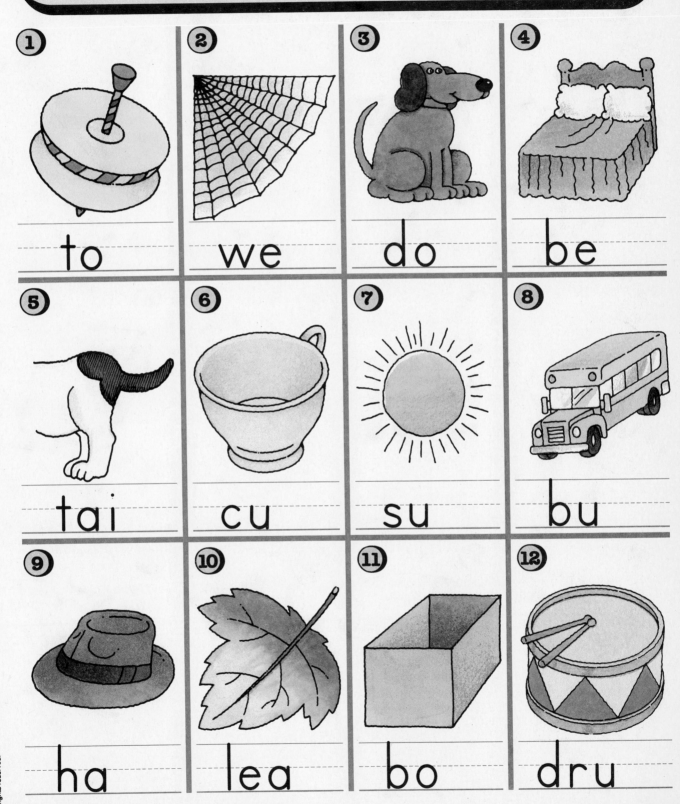

1. to
2. we
3. do
4. be
5. tai
6. cu
7. su
8. bu
9. ha
10. lea
11. bo
12. dru

LESSON 4: Final consonants

9

Here's what to do! Say the name of each picture. Print the letter for its ending sound.

1

2

3

4

5

6

7

8

9

10

11

12

Now try this! Say the name of each picture. If you hear the consonant at the beginning, circle it on the left. If you hear it at the end, circle it on the right.

1. s   s
2. d   d
3. g   g
4. h   h
5. f   f
6. p   p
7. r   r
8. m   m
9. k   k
10. y   y
11. t   t
12. j   j
13. w   w
14. b   b
15. n   n

LESSON 5: Initial and final consonants

Here's what to do!

Say the name of each picture. Print the letters for its beginning and ending sounds.

1.   o

2.   a

3.   u

4.   e

5.   u

6.   o

7.   i

8.   a

9.   e

Here's what to do!
Say the name of each picture. Print the letter for its middle sound.

1. d

2.

3.

4.

5.

6.

7.

8.

9.

10.

11.

12.

LESSON 6: Medial consonants

13

Here's what to do! Say the name of each picture. Print the letter for its middle sound.

① ra __ io

② spi __ er

③ ti __ er

④ pea __ ut

⑤ **7** se __ en

⑥ ca __ el

Now try this! Say the name of each picture. Print its missing letter. Do what the sentences tell you to do.

①

Can you see a dra _____ on?

Color the dra _____ on red.

②

I can see the ca _____ in.

Color the ca _____ in brown.

③

I need the bo _____ es.

Color the bo _____ es blue.

④

Jan licked a le _____ on.

Color the le _____ on yellow.

Try this! Say the name of each picture. Print its missing letter. Do what the sentences tell you to do.

1

Pam will pull the wa _____ on.

Color the wa _____ on red.

2

The _____ un is hot.

Color the _____ un yellow.

3

The boat has a sai _____

Color the sai _____ green.

4

Play the ra _____ io.

Color the ra _____ io blue.

5

Gus can take a _____ us ride.

Color the _____ us yellow.

6

A bug is on the lea _____ .

Color the lea _____ green.

7

Can the ro _____ ot run?

Color the ro _____ ot red.

8

Ken will spin the _____ op.

Color the _____ op blue.

Here's what to do! Say the name of each picture. Print the letters for its beginning, middle, and ending sounds.

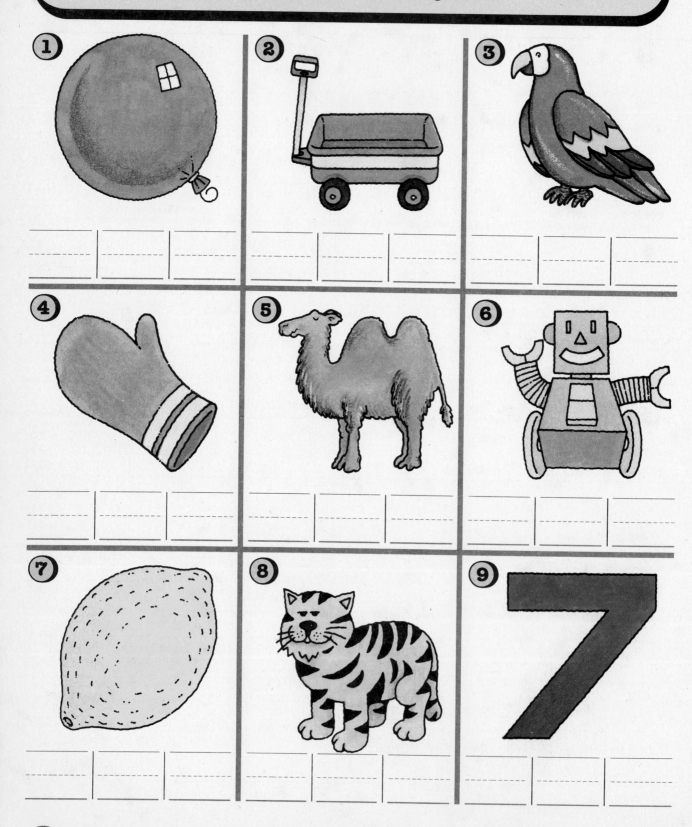

LESSON 7: Initial, medial, and final consonants

Here's what to do! Circle the name of each picture.

If a word or syllable has only one vowel, and it comes at the beginning or between two consonants, the vowel is usually short.

①

hat   ham

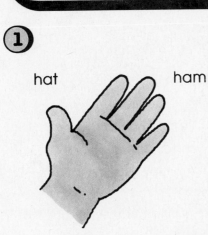

hand   had

②

bag   hat

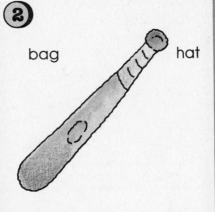

bat   bad

③

camp   lad

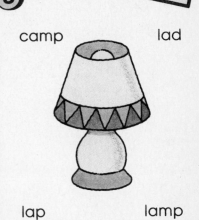

lap   lamp

④

sad   back

bag   bat

⑤

cat   cap

cab   can

⑥

and   an

at   ant

⑦

mat   man

pan   map

⑧

cat   can

cab   cap

⑨

mad   ram

rack   mat

LESSON 8: Short vowel A   **17**

Here's what to do! Circle the rhyming words in each box. Draw a picture of the word that does not rhyme.

1

cat

fan

hat

mat

2

Max

tax

bag

wax

3

cap

tap

map

cab

4

sack

hand

back

tack

5

bag

rag

cap

tag

6

sand

land

pan

band

7

ham

fan

ran

can

8

sad

bat

bad

had

9

quack

cat

sack

back

10

hand

land

lamp

sand

11

pan

fan

Dan

hat

12

sat

ax

pat

fat

Here's what to do! Print the name of each picture. Print a word that rhymes with it. Do what the sentences tell you to do.

① Color the bag red.

② Color the fan green.

③ Color the cap red.

④ Color the ax blue.

⑤ Color the cat black.

⑥ Color the tack yellow.

⑦ Color the lamp green and blue.

⑧ Color the ram black and yellow.

Here's what to do! Fill in the bubble beside the word that will finish each sentence.

1 I am Sam and my _____ is Pat.   ○ camp   ○ cat   ○ cart

2 She likes pats so I named her _____ .   ○ that   ○ last   ○ ran

3 Pat _____ up milk and cat food.   ○ class   ○ sat   ○ laps

4 She eats a lot but she is not _____ .   ○ van   ○ fat   ○ lamp

5 She likes to lick my _____ .   ○ hand   ○ gas   ○ band

6 Pat is not _____ to have a bath.   ○ gap   ○ glad   ○ rack

7 She runs as _____ as she can.   ○ fast   ○ class   ○ bass

8 I _____ always find her.   ○ can   ○ past   ○ fast

9 She takes a nap on a _____ .   ○ mast   ○ mat   ○ map

10 Sometimes she naps in my _____ .   ○ park   ○ camp   ○ cap

11 I am so happy that _____ is my cat.   ○ Mark   ○ Pat   ○ Ann

Here's what to do! Circle the name of each picture.

If a word or syllable has only one vowel, and it comes at the beginning or between two consonants, the vowel is usually short.

①
silk
milk
mill
bill

②
mitt
bit
fit
mill

③
wind
pig
wig
fix

④
tips
lips
dips
dill

⑤
big
pig
fig
pit

⑥
hill
bill
sill
mitt

⑦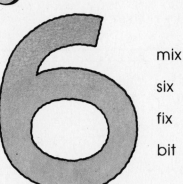
mix
six
fix
bit

⑧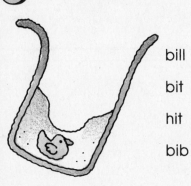
bill
bit
hit
bib

⑨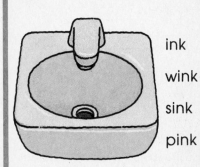
ink
wink
sink
pink

LESSON 10: Short vowel I 21

Try this! Use the same color to color the parts of each ball with rhyming words.

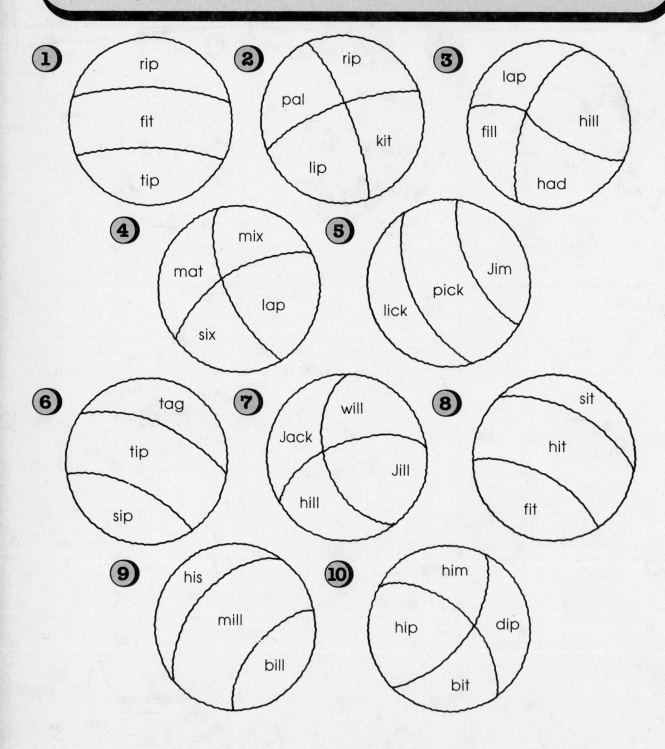

1. rip, fit, tip

2. rip, pal, kit, lip

3. lap, fill, hill, had

4. mix, mat, lap, six

5. Jim, pick, lick

6. tag, tip, sip

7. will, Jack, Jill, hill

8. sit, hit, fit

9. his, mill, bill

10. him, hip, dip, bit

Do it this way! Print the name of each picture. Print a word that rhymes with it.

① ② ③ ④

⑤ ⑥ ⑦ ⑧

LESSON 11: Short vowel I

23

Here's what to do! Circle the word that answers each riddle.
Print it on the line.

1 It can swim.
What is it?

fish

fist   fish

fix   fit

2 It fits on a pot.
What is it?

lip   lit

lid   list

3 It comes after five.
What is it?

6

dish   dim

did   six

4 Jack and Jill ran up it.
What is it?

hit   hip

hill   him

5 Lunch goes on it.
What is it?

dill   dish

dig   dip

6 It has a funny tail.
What is it?

pin   pig

pill   pit

7 It fits on a finger.
What is it?

rip   rid

rig   ring

8 Baby needs this.
What is it?

bib   bid

bill   bit

9 We play with it.
What is it?

mint   mitt

mill   mix

Here's what to do! Read the words that begin each sentence.
Use all of the words to finish the sentence.

1 _____

It is time to _____ .

| a |
| trip |
| plan |

2 _____

We will camp _____ .

| Will |
| Uncle |
| with |

3 _____

Pam can _____ .

| a |
| find |
| map |

4 _____

Zack and Pam will _____ .

| snacks |
| the |
| fix |

5 _____

What will we pack _____ ?

| in |
| bags |
| our |

6 _____

Will our bags fit _____ ?

| in |
| van |
| the |

7 _____

Our dog Wags _____ .

| will |
| tag |
| along |

8 _____

The trip we take _____ .

| fun |
| be |
| will |

LESSON 12: Short vowels A and I 25

Here's what to do! Circle the word that will finish each sentence. Print it on the line.

1. I am fishing ____ Uncle Jim.

   _____   him   with   gift

2. We ____ to catch a basket of fish.

   _____   hand   van   plan

3. I put a ____ worm on my hook.

   _____   bag   fat   tack

4. I think I see a fish ____ by.

   _____   dish   swish   mitt

5. I feel a tug on my line at ____ .

   _____   fast   last   pat

6. A fish just ____ my bait.

   _____   sift   fix   bit

7. It is so big I can hardly ____ it.

   _____   lid   limb   lift

8. Uncle Jim helps me pull it ____ .

   _____   last   in   fill

9. This ____ will make a nice big meal.

   _____   fish   wish   fins

10. It is too big to fit in one ____ .

   _____   inch   dish   it

11. Now we ____ fix fish and chips.

   _____   can   cast   caps

LESSON 12: Short vowels A and I

_____

- - - - - - - - - - - - - - - - - -

_____

Here's what to do! Circle the name of each picture. Print the vowel you hear in the word you circled.

If a word or syllable has only one vowel, and it comes at the beginning or between two consonants, the vowel is usually short.

①

cap   cup

kit   _____

②

gas   gull

gum   _____

③

Dick   duck

dad   _____

④

can   cup

cap   _____

⑤

as   bun

bus   _____

⑥

tug   tip

bug   _____

⑦

but   nuts

nap   _____

⑧

sun   sum

dim   _____

⑨

tab   bin

bat   _____

LESSON 13: Short vowel U

27

Here's what to do! Find the word in the box that names each picture. Print in on the line.

bun	cup	rug	bus	bug	sun
gum	hug	hut	tub	jug	duck

① _____

② _____

③ _____

④ _____

⑤ _____

⑥ _____

⑦ _____

⑧ _____

⑨ _____

⑩ _____

⑪ _____

⑫ _____

Here's what to do!

Circle the word that answers each riddle. Print it on the line.

1 I can hide in a jug.
What am I?

bus   tub
sun   bug

2 I am good to eat.
What am I?

dug   bun
fun   run

3 This is fun to do.
What is it?

just   lump
muff   jump

4 This is quick to do.
What is it?

fun   run
bun   cup

5 You can ride in me.
What am I?

bud   bug
bus   us

6 I shine on you.
What am I?

sun   but
run   fun

7 I say, "Quack, quack."
What am I?

tuck   luck
pup   duck

8 You can eat me.
What am I?

cut   but
fun   nut

9 We like to chew it.
What is it?

just   but
gum   must

Here's what to do! Circle the word that will finish each sentence. Print it on the line.

1 _____

There was a fuss on the _____ .

| run |
| bus |
| must |

2 _____

It was _____ a fuss about a bug.

| just |
| bug |
| bus |

3 _____

A _____ jumped on Gus.

| rug |
| hug |
| bug |

4 _____

Gus jumped _____ .

| run |
| cup |
| up |

5 _____

The bug jumped on _____ .

| sun |
| run |
| Bunny |

6 _____

I had to _____ for the bug.

| must |
| lump |
| jump |

7 _____

I got the bug and put it in a _____ .

| fun |
| jug |
| rust |

8 _____

The bug fuss on the bus was _____ .

| rust |
| fun |
| cup |

Try this! Make new words by changing the vowels. Print them on the lines.

a	i	u

① fan   fin

② bad

③ ham

④ hat

⑤ as

⑥ bag

⑦ rag

1. Is a big cup a little nut? ○ Yes ○ No

2. Is the sun black? ○ Yes ○ No

3. Can a cat run fast? ○ Yes ○ No

4. Can a big pig sing for you? ○ Yes ○ No

5. Can we nap in a tan van? ○ Yes ○ No

6. Can a man run up a hill? ○ Yes ○ No

7. Is a green rug red? ○ Yes ○ No

8. Can you sit on a bus? ○ Yes ○ No

9. Can a little cup run fast and jump? ○ Yes ○ No

10. Can you fill a pan with milk? ○ Yes ○ No

11. Can a doll jump on the bus? ○ Yes ○ No

12. Can a pig go as fast as a cab? ○ Yes ○ No

13. Can you rub your hands? ○ Yes ○ No

14. Is a happy cat sad? ○ Yes ○ No

15. Can a bus be big? ○ Yes ○ No

16. Can a bug sit in the mud? ○ Yes ○ No

17. Can a hug nap on a rug? ○ Yes ○ No

Here's what to do! Find the word in the box that names each picture. Print it on the line.

If a word or syllable has only one vowel, and it comes at the beginning or between two consonants, the vowel is usually short.

| top | mop | pot | box | Tom | sock |
| dot | doll | fox | lock | rock | pop |

1.

2.

3.

4.

5.

6.

7.

8.

9.

10.

11.

12.

LESSON 16: Short vowel O   33

1.
fix
cob
fox
six

2.
pot
top
tap
pit

3.
bill
sill
dill
doll

4.
cot
dot
job
cut

5.
dug
dog
dig
pot

6.
rock
sit
sack
sock

7.
pig
pop
pup
pat

8.
lag
log
bug
lot

9.
luck
lock
lick
lack

Try this!

Fill in the bubble beside the sentence that tells about each picture. Draw a box around each short **O** word in the sentences.

1

- ◯ The fox is not on the log.
- ◯ The fox is in the log.
- ◯ The fox is on the log.
- ◯ The fox is under the log.

2

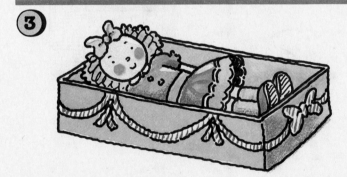

- ◯ Rob lost his socks.
- ◯ Rob sat on a big rock.
- ◯ Rob is on the big log.
- ◯ Rob has a big rock in his hand.

3

- ◯ The dog ran to the box.
- ◯ The mop is not in the box.
- ◯ I will hop on the log.
- ◯ See the doll in the box.

4

- ◯ I got the mop for Dot.
- ◯ Jill has got a big top.
- ◯ The big top is on the mop.
- ◯ The red top is in Bob's hand.

Here's what to do! Circle the name of each picture.

1
six   fix

sit   sun

2
bun   hit

box   fox

3
tan   fan

fun   fin

4
cup   cap

kit   can

5
sick   sock

son   sack

6
rock   luck

lock   sock

7
fix   fox

box   fun

8
pin   top

pot   tip

9
pot   dug

dog   log

Here's what to do! Print the name of each picture on the line.

1.

2.

3.

4.

5.

6.

7.

8.

9.

10.

11.

12.

LESSON 18: Reviewing short vowels A, I, U, O

37

1 What does Dot have in her _____ ?

2 Pam hopes it is full of _____ .

3 Bob _____ hot dogs.

4 Uncle _____ wants buns.

5 All the _____ want popcorn.

Gus
kids
pot
wants
nuts

---

1 There is a slick _____ and Dot can't stop.

2 She _____ and drops the pot.

3 The pot was _____ of soup.

4 When she slipped, _____ slopped.

5 Now we have to get the _____ !

slips
it
mop
spot
full

Try **this!** Print the name of each picture on the line with the same number.

If a word or syllable has only one vowel, and it comes at the beginning or between two consonants, the vowel is usually short.

(1) _____

(2) _____

(3) _____

(4) _____

(5) _____

(6) _____

(7) _____

(8) _____

(9) _____

(10) _____

(11) _____

(12) _____

LESSON 19: Short vowel E

39

Here's what to do! Do what the sentences tell you to do.
Print the name of each picture.

1 Find the bed.
Color it red and blue.

2 Find the jet.
Color it black.

3 Find the nest.
Color three eggs red and
two eggs blue.

4 See the tent.
Color it yellow.

5 See the belt.
Color it green.

6 Find the vest.
Color it red and black.

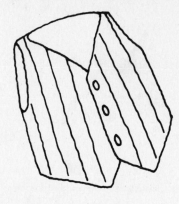
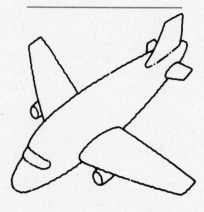

_____   _____

_____   _____

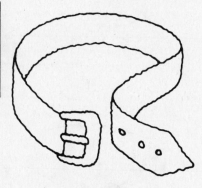
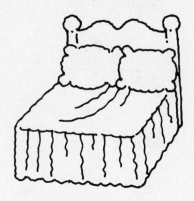

_____   _____

_____   _____

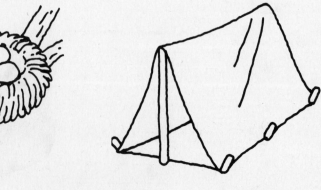

_____   _____

_____   _____

Do it this way!

Fill in the bubble below the word that will finish each sentence.

1. My name is _____ .

   men ○   Jeff ○   jet ○

2. I want to get a _____ .

   bet ○   pet ○   yet ○

3. I would like a pet dog _____ .

   rest ○   west ○   best ○

4. I will _____ take care of my pet.

   help ○   bell ○   nest ○

5. I can take it to the _____ .

   vet ○   bet ○   set ○

6. I will make sure it is _____ .

   get ○   fed ○   bed ○

7. It will need a good _____ .

   bed ○   nest ○   best ○

8. I will _____ it in and out.

   jet ○   test ○   let ○

9. I can dry it when it's _____ .

   net ○   wet ○   set ○

10. I will _____ it if I get it.

    sled ○   pet ○   west ○

11. I might name my pet _____ .

    Pepper ○   fed ○   set ○

① ② ③ ④ ⑤

Now try this! Answer each sentence by printing **yes** or **no** on the line.

① You can rest in a bed.

② I have ten fingers and ten toes.

③ A cat has six legs.

④ A big bus can jump up and down.

⑤ You can go fast in a jet.

⑥ An ant is as big as an ox.

⑦ Six is less than ten.

⑧ You can sit in a tent.

Here's what to do! Find the word that will finish each sentence.
Print it on the line.

1. A crab can rest in the _____ .

2. A hen rests on a _____ .

3. A _____ can rest in a pen.

4. A spider rests in a _____ .

5. A bug can be snug in a _____ .

nest

rug

web

sand

pig

---

1. _____ rest in their beds.

2. It is _____ to rest in a tent.

3. I _____ rest best in my own bed.

4. My _____ likes to rest there, too.

5. I can sleep like a _____ and so can my dog.

fun

log

dog

can

Kids

Try this! Change the vowel to make a new word. Print it on the line.

1 _____
tug _____

2 _____
tab _____

3 _____
fox _____

4 _____
rust _____

5 _____
sand _____

6 _____
tint _____

Now try this! Find the word that will finish each sentence. Print it on the line.

1 After the rain, out came the _____ .

2 I _____ out to play and have fun.

3 When I hopped I slid in the _____ .

4 I _____ and landed with a thud.

5 Now I am covered _____ mud.

6 It is time to _____ in the tub.

hop
with
sun
fell
ran
mud

Here's what to do! Find the word that will finish each sentence. Print it on the line.

If one syllable has two vowels, the first vowel is usually long, and the second is silent.

cave

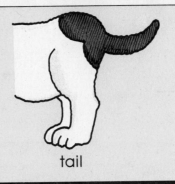
tail

rake

1 Jane made a _____ when she saw it rain.

2 She wanted the rain to go _____ .

3 She had planned to _____ outside with Jake.

4 Then Jake _____ to play inside with Jane.

away
face
came
play

1 They had to _____ for the rain to stop.

2 While they waited they played _____ .

3 They baked a cake and _____ a piece.

4 At last the _____ stopped and out they ran.

games
rain
wait
ate

LESSON 22: Long vowel A   **45**

Here's what to do! Circle the word that will finish each sentence. Print it on the line.

1 May we go to the
_____ today?

_____

bake   take   lake

2 It is a nice day to _____
our boat.

_____

pail   sail   mail

3 We could _____ sand
castles on the beach.

_____

make   wake   fake

4 We all like to _____ in the
waves.

_____

save   play   take

5 Is there any _____ we can
go today?

_____

say   tail   way

Now try this! Circle each long **A** word in the box. Print the name of each picture on the line.

tap	tape	cap	cape	at	ate
mail	mat	rain	gate	hay	ham

1

_____

2

_____

3

_____

4

_____

Here's what to do! Circle the name of each picture.

1	2	3	4
fin fire	pig pile	bike big	bib bite

Now try this! Circle the word that will finish each sentence. Print it on the line.

1

Mike likes to ride a _____ .

bit   bike   bite

2

Diane likes to _____ .

hike   hill   hit

3

Ike likes cherry _____ .

pie   pig   pike

4

Kyle likes to play on a _____ .

bite   hive   slide

5

Fido likes to take a _____ .

rid   ride   hive

6

We all like lunch _____ .

tire   time   tip

LESSON 23: Long vowel I   47

Here's what to do! Circle the word that will finish each sentence. Print it on the line.

1 A turtle can _____ inside its shell.

dime   time   hide

2 A _____ can hide in a den very well.

lion   tile   pie

3 My dog can hide behind our _____ .

likes   bikes   ties

4 A spider can hide anywhere it _____ .

pine   mine   likes

5 I like to hide any _____ anywhere.

time   ride   fire

6 I hope no one will _____ me there.

kind   find   pile

Now try this! Circle each long I word in the box. Print the name of each picture on the line.

dim	dime	pin	pine	rid	ride
mine	tie	sit	kite	nine	fire

1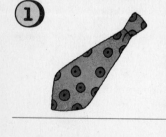

2

3

4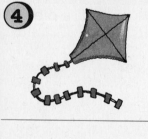

1 We did it in a race.   rain   ran   man

2 A dog can wag it.   tail   pail   pat

3 We did it to Pat's cake.   at   late   ate

4 Jane has a can of it.   pat   pain   paint

5 We like to ride boats on this.   bake   mile   lake

6 We like to eat it.   bit   pie   pat

7 We can ride it.   bill   bat   bike

8 We do this to shoes.   tip   tie   time

9 We can save this.   like   dime   dip

10 A wet day has this.   rain   rate   ran

Kay

Mike

Here's what to do!

Circle the answer Yes or No for each sentence. Circle all the long **U** words you find. Print them on the lines.

1. A red vase is blue. Yes No

2. We can wash in a tube. Yes No

3. A baby lion is a cube. Yes No

4. A mule has nine tails. Yes No

5. Music is fun to sing and play. Yes No

6. We can eat a suit. Yes No

7. A rule is a top that can sing. Yes No

8. We play a song with a flute. Yes No

9. We can hum a tune. Yes No

Do it this way! Read the words in the box.
Print the short **U** words under Short **U**. Print
the long **U** words under Long **U**.

If one syllable has two vowels, the first vowel is usually long, and the second is silent.

Short **U**	Long **U**

cute

must

bug

duck

jump

suit

tune

bump

tube

dug

cube

mule

nut

fuse

use

hum

52   **LESSON 25: Long vowel U**

Do it this way! Read each word. If the word has a long vowel, fill in the bubble beside **long.** If the word has a short vowel, fill in the bubble beside **short.**

1 late ○ long ○ short

2 June ○ long ○ short

3 mule ○ long ○ short

4 man ○ long ○ short

5 tube ○ long ○ short

6 ride ○ long ○ short

7 rain ○ long ○ short

8 pick ○ long ○ short

9 six ○ long ○ short

10 use ○ long ○ short

11 cute ○ long ○ short

12 cap ○ long ○ short

13 bat ○ long ○ short

14 time ○ long ○ short

15 fun ○ long ○ short

16 bake ○ long ○ short

17 lick ○ long ○ short

18 us ○ long ○ short

19 map ○ long ○ short

20 wide ○ long ○ short

21 gate ○ long ○ short

22 wipe ○ long ○ short

23 pie ○ long ○ short

24 tune ○ long ○ short

25 lap ○ long ○ short

26 ate ○ long ○ short

27 nut ○ long ○ short

28 up ○ long ○ short

29 fire ○ long ○ short

30 make ○ long ○ short

1 We ____ to play music.   ride   like   hike

2 It is a nice ____ to spend a day.   pay   side   way

3 June likes to play her ____ .   flute   suit   time

4 Hugh can ____ his tuba.   bake   use   fuse

5 Mike ____ tunes on his uke.   side   sit   plays

6 Sue plays a ____ .   bugle   suit   like

7 ____ like to play my drum.   It   I   Ice

8 We all sing ____ .   tunes   times   tire

9 Some ____ we hope to get blue uniforms.   tip   cub   time

10 We want to play ____ in a parade.   music   suit   fan

Do it this way! Circle each long **O** word in the box.

If one syllable has two vowels, the first vowel is usually long, and the second is silent.

rod	road	rode	cot	coat	got	goat
hope	hop	robe	rob	row	cost	coast

Now try this! Find the missing word for each sentence. Print it on the line.

(1) Rover woke up when the sun _____ on his doghouse.

(2) He poked his _____ into his bowl.

(3) He hoped to find a _____ .

(4) There was no bone in his _____ .

(5) Just then along came his _____ Joe.

(6) Something poked out of his _____ .

(7) Joe said, "I have something to _____ you."

(8) Oh, boy! It was a bone for _____ !

coat
shone
owner
Rover
show
bone
bowl
nose

LESSON 27: Long vowel O 55

Here's what to do! Circle the name of each picture.

① cot   coat

② toad   tad

③ got   goat

④ note   not

⑤ sap   soap

⑥ rope   rot

Now try this! The missing word for each sentence rhymes with the word in the box. Print the word that will finish each sentence on the line.

① Joe got in his boat to _____ .

bow

② Joe's _____ Rover wanted to go, too.

fog

③ Rover poked Joe with his _____ .

rose

④ Then he hopped like a _____ .

road

⑤ Joe said, "You can _____ if you will sit still."

no

Here's what to do! Find the name of each picture in the box.
Print it on the line.

tail	soap	cube	five	kite
bake	tube	dive	hope	toad

1. _____

2. _____

3. _____

4. _____

5. _____

6. _____

Now try this! Find the word that will finish each sentence. Print it on the line.

1. Ruth likes to make _____ sandwiches.

2. Sue mixes fruit juice with _____ cubes.

3. Jake bakes carrot _____ .

4. It's fun to make our _____ lunch.

cake

own

ice

tuna

LESSON 28: Reviewing long vowels A, I, U, O

Here's what to do! Fill in the bubble beside the word that will finish each sentence.

1 Tim went outside and had a nice _____ .

- ○ Tim
- ○ time

2 He _____ his bike and flew his kite.

- ○ rode
- ○ rod

3 He played _____ and seek with June.

- ○ hid
- ○ hide

4 Then they came in and _____ cookies.

- ○ mad
- ○ made

5 They _____ every single bite.

- ○ ate
- ○ at

6 They each made a paper _____ .

- ○ plan
- ○ plane

7 They decided to _____ grape juice to make ice cubes.

- ○ use
- ○ us

8 Tim's grape ice _____ tasted great!

- ○ cub
- ○ cube

9 They played _____ the tail on the paper pig.

- ○ pine
- ○ pin

10 _____ had a nice time inside, too.

- ○ Tim
- ○ time

LESSON 28: Reviewing long vowels A, I, U, O

Give this a try! Circle the name of each picture.

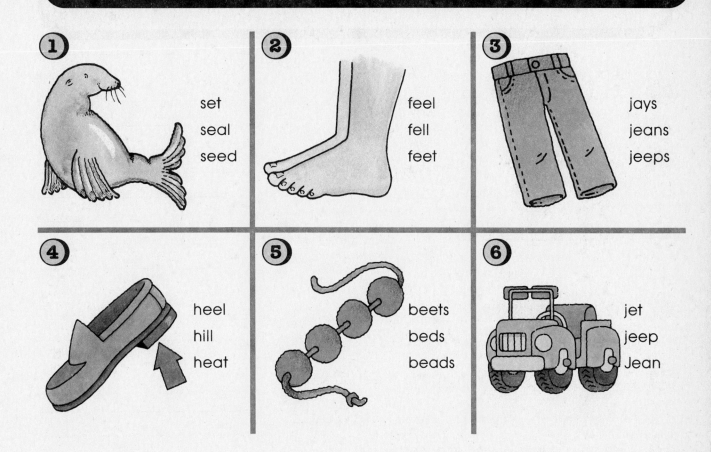

1
set
seal
seed

2
feel
fell
feet

3
jays
jeans
jeeps

4
heel
hill
heat

5
beets
beds
beads

6
jet
jeep
Jean

Now try this! Circle the word that will finish each sentence. Print it on the line.

1 Seals live in the _____ .   seat   sea   set

2 They _____ fish for their meals.   beans   eat   feet

3 We can teach _____ to do tricks.   east   seals   beets

4 A real seal show is a treat to _____ .   green   free   see

Do it this way! Circle the long **E** word in each sentence. Print it on the line.

1. I wore my new blue jeans.

2. I wanted them to stay clean.

3. It was hard for me to do.

4. My dog got dirty feet on them.

5. The bus splashed mud from the street on them.

6. I sat on a gummy seat with them.

7. My lunch box leaked on them.

8. At lunch pea soup slopped on them.

9. Gus dropped his beans on top of them.

10. After that, well, so much for my jeans.

11. They were the biggest mess I've ever seen!

LESSON 29: Long vowel E

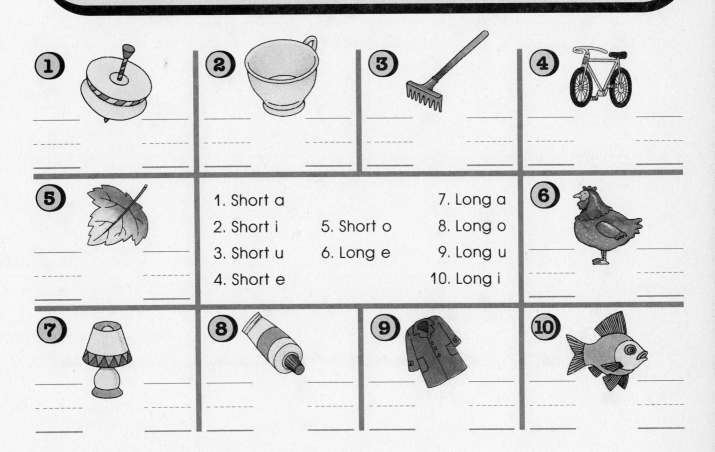

Try this! Say the name of each picture. Print the vowel you hear on the first line. Find a picture for each sound on the list. Print its number on the second line.

1. Short a
2. Short i
3. Short u
4. Short e
5. Short o
6. Long e
7. Long a
8. Long o
9. Long u
10. Long i

Now try this! Finish the rhyming words.

1 hat mat sat

2 went d___ r___

3 fun r___ b___

4 gate l___ d___

5 like b___ h___

6 goat c___ b___

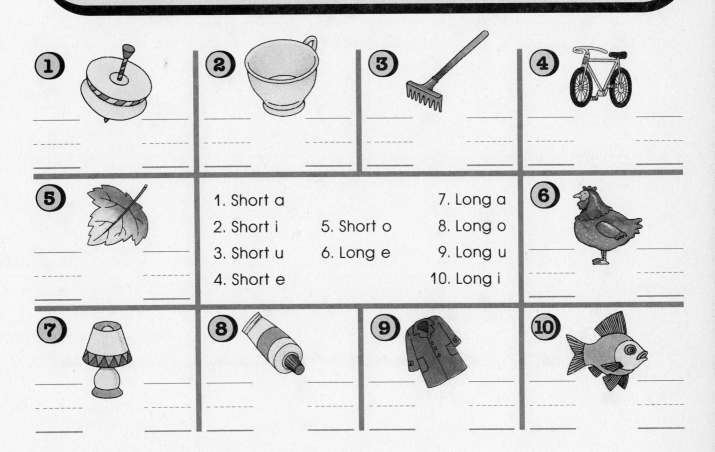

LESSON 30: Reviewing long and short vowels and rhyming words

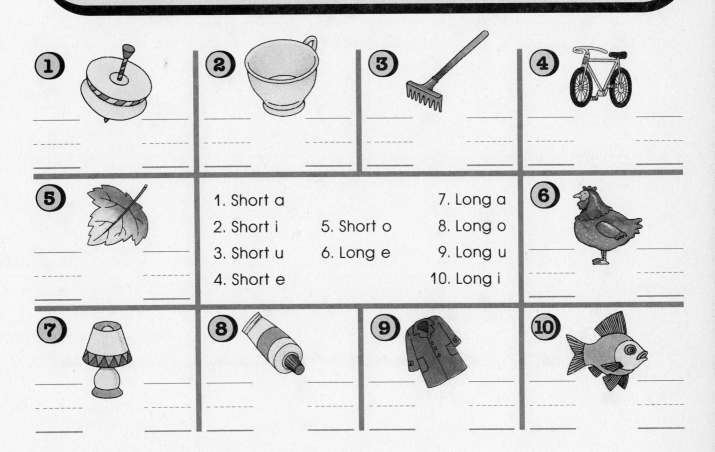

Do it this way! Change the first vowel in each word to make a new word. Print it on the line.

1 boat _____

2 sod _____

3 red _____

4 oar _____

5 hop _____

6 ran _____

7 cone _____

8 wide _____

9 bake _____

10 nip _____

11 tame _____

12 map _____

Now do this! Find a word in the box that rhymes with each word. Print it on the line.

1 time _____

2 cube _____

3 rub _____

4 need _____

5 tape _____

6 bat _____

| tube |
| cub |
| cape |
| dime |
| hat |
| feed |

1 seat _____

2 fin _____

3 hope _____

4 bet _____

5 rob _____

6 toad _____

| tin |
| road |
| cob |
| rope |
| get |
| heat |

LESSON 30: Reviewing long and short vowels and rhyming words

Give this a try! Say the name of each picture. Print the vowel you hear on the line. Circle **short** if the vowel is short. Circle **long** if it is long.

1. short   long
2. short   long
3. short   long
4. short   long
5. short   long
6. short   long
7. short   long
8. short   long
9. short   long
10. short   long
11. short   long
12. short   long

LESSON 31: Reviewing long and short vowels   63

Here's what to do! Circle the missing word for each sentence. Print it on the line.

1 I have a _____ named Wags.

fog   dog   day

2 His _____ always wags.

tap   tape   tail

3 He _____ dog food by the bags.

eats   ears   east

4 His tummy is _____ and sags.

bite   big   kite

5 His ears are long _____ flags.

like   lime   lit

6 Wags and I like to _____ .

fat   way   play

7 I _____ him to go one way.

fell   tell   beet

8 He always _____ the other way.

toes   got   goes

9 He would never really _____ away.

fun   run   fuse

10 Wags is _____ and I like him that way.

cute   cut   cat

Do it this way! Put two words together to make a new word.
Print the new word on the line.

1

pea weed
sea nut

seaweed

2

meal oat
my   self

3

cup rain
coat cake

4

be   rail
road may

5

base class
mate ball

6

pack corn
back pop

LESSON 32: Vowels in compound words

Give this a try! Look at each picture. Read the two words below it. Put them together to make one new word that names the picture. Print it on the line.

 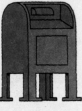

1.

A box for mail is a _____ .

mail + box

2.

A coat for rain is a _____ .

rain + coat

3.

A pack for your back is a _____ .

back + pack

4.

A boat with a sail is a _____ .

sail + boat

5.

Corn that can pop is _____ .

pop + corn

Here's what to do! Say the name of each picture. Circle each vowel you hear. Print the number of syllables you hear.

Many words are made of small parts called syllables.
Each syllable has one vowel sound.

c(a)t = 1 syllable   k(i)t t(e)n = 2 syllables

① b(a)s k(e)t   2

② m i t t e n s

③ s t e p s

④ p e n c i l

⑤ t e n t

⑥ p u p p e t

⑦ t r u n k

⑧ r o b o t

⑨ r u l e r

| basket | | kitten | | baby |
| button | | | seven | |

1 Molly got a _____ named Popcorn.

2 Popcorn was only _____ weeks old.

3 He had a nose like a _____ .

4 Molly made a bed for Popcorn in a _____ .

5 Popcorn was like a little _____ .

Give this a try! Say the name of each picture. If it has a soft **C,** circle the picture. If it has a hard **C,** color it.

When **c** is followed by **e, i,** or **y,** it usually has a soft sound.

①

face

②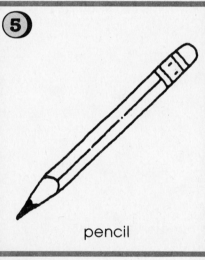

cap

③

clock

④

cup

⑤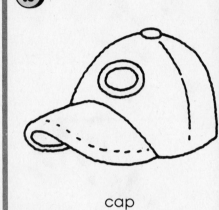

pencil

⑥

cake

⑦

mice

⑧

dice

⑨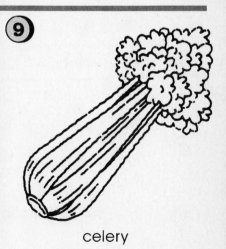

celery

LESSON 34: Hard and soft C

69

Here's what to do! Circle the word that will finish each
sentence. Print it on the line.

1 Cindy and Vince will run in
a _____ .

_____

_____

mice   race

nice   next

2 They both hope to win
first _____ .

_____

_____

nice   race

place   slice

3 They make sure the _____ of
their shoes are tied.

_____

_____

rice   laces

nice   price

4 They race to the _____ .

_____

_____

next   nice

fence   celery

5 It's a tie! They both
win _____ prizes.

_____

_____

mice   cereal

nice   price

6 Both Cindy and Vince have
smiling _____ .

_____

_____

lace   faces

race   space

Here's what to do! Say the name of each picture. If the name has a soft **G**, circle the picture. If it has a hard **G**, color it.

When **g** is followed by **e, i,** or **y**, it usually has a soft sound.

1.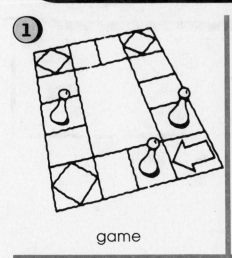
game

2.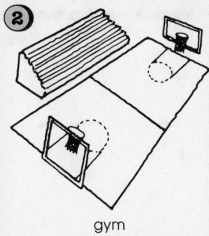
gym

3.
goat

4.
page

5.
giant

6.
gum

7.
dragon

8.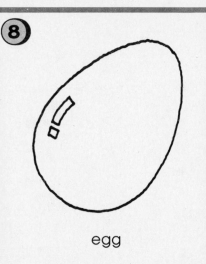
egg

9.
giraffe

LESSON 35: Hard and soft G

71

Do it this way! The letter **G** can make a hard or a soft sound. Read the words in the box. Listen for the sounds of **G**. Print the words under Soft **G** or Hard **G**.

When **g** is followed by **e, i,** or **y**, it usually has a soft sound.

gem	age	dog	cage	good	gum
gave	goat	stage	wag	page	wage
gym		giant	egg		game

Soft **G** words	Hard **G** words

Try this! Draw a green line under each hard **C** or **G** word. Print each soft **C** or **G** word in a large leaf.

price
mice
goat
age
wage
games
huge
cent
gem
ice
gym
cake
race
rice
gas
cone
face
giant

LESSON 36: Hard and soft C and G

Here's what to do! Print **S** beside the soft **C** or **G** words.
Print **H** beside the hard **C** or **G** words.

1 nice _____

2 cuff _____

3 ice _____

4 cabin _____

5 lunge _____

6 camel _____

7 game _____

8 race _____

9 gull _____

10 age _____

11 came _____

12 coast _____

13 cake _____

14 coat _____

15 pencil _____

16 gym _____

17 cent _____

18 giant _____

19 gate _____

20 ridge _____

21 care _____

22 goes _____

23 recess _____

24 Vince _____

25 page _____

26 mice _____

27 rice _____

28 gem _____

29 Gail _____

30 gum _____

Now do this! Draw a red box around each soft **G** word. Draw a blue circle around each soft **C** word.

1 A giraffe is a gentle giant.

2 You can tell by its kind face.

3 A giraffe is taller than most ceilings.

4 Zoos with giraffes need tall fences.

5 Giraffes think large leaves are delicious.

6 Cereal and vegetables make nice giraffe treats.

7 I am saving my cents to see them at the zoo.

_____

- - - - - - - - - - - - - - -

_____

Give this a try! Say the name of each picture. Print its beginning blend.

A **blend** is two or three consonants sounded together.

① apes

② og

③ ee

④ ain

Now try this! Use the words to answer the riddles.

① I can jump and hop.
You find me in a pond.
I eat bugs.

_____

I am a _____ .

② I am green.
You can find me in a park.
Birds live in me.

_____

I am a _____ .

③ I can be small or big.
I make a good toy.
I run on a track.

_____

I am a _____ .

④ We grow on vines.
We come in bunches.
We are good to eat.

_____

We are _____ .

LESSON 37: R Blends

75

① grapes
grass
grade

② trim
truck
train

③ trade
trap
tree

④ drive
drum
drink

⑤ from
frost
fruit

⑥ train
truck
trick

⑦ dress
drapes
drum

⑧ gray
grass
grab

Now do this! Find the blend in each word. Print it on the line.

① bring _____

② brave _____

③ cross _____

④ fry _____

⑤ trick _____

⑥ brick _____

⑦ trip _____

⑧ grain _____

⑨ trade _____

⑩ grade _____

⑪ bride _____

⑫ free _____

⑬ drive _____

⑭ crumb _____

⑮ price _____

Give this a try! Say the name of each picture. Print its beginning blend on the line.

1. _____

2. _____

3. _____

4. _____

5. _____

6. _____

Now try this! Circle the word that will finish each sentence. Print it on the line.

1. At night I went to _____.

   _____   slap   sleep

2. When I woke up I saw a _____ of snow.

   _____   blanket   blue

3. The snow was like a white _____ .

   _____   clap   cloud

4. It covered the trees and _____ .

   _____   plops   plants

5. I covered my hands with my _____ .

   _____   gloves   flag

6. I went out to _____ in the snow.

   _____   plants   play

_____

- - - - - - - - - - - - - - - - - - - -

Do it this way! Print the answer for each riddle. The pictures will help you.

1 Sometimes I ring. Sometimes I chime. I tick-tock all the time.

_____

- - - - - - - - - - - -

_____

2 High up on a pole I go. With the wind I flap and blow.

_____

- - - - - - - - - - - -

_____

3 I hold your food. Look for me under your hot dog.

_____

- - - - - - - - - - - -

_____

4 I stick things for you. I stick to you, too.

_____

- - - - - - - - - - - -

_____

Now do this! Find the missing word for each sentence in the box. Print it on the line.

_____

- - - - - - - - - - - -

1 I have a new magnifying _____ .

_____

- - - - - - - - - - - -

2 When I hold it _____ to things they get bigger.

_____

- - - - - - - - - - - -

3 A blade of _____ looks like a tree trunk.

- - - - - - - - - - - -

_____

4 _____ of wood are really full of holes.

_____

- - - - - - - - - - - -

5 A _____ looks like a big black monster!

| Blocks |
| grass |
| fly |
| close |
| glass |

Here's what to do! Say the name of each picture. Print its beginning blend.

1.

2.

3.

4.

5.

6.

7.

8.

9.

Give this a try! Print the name of each picture on the line.

① ② ③ ④

Now try this! Circle the word that will finish each sentence. Print it on the line.

① A big black ____
comes to my window.

_____

from   crow   frost

② Crows eat bugs in the
____ .

_____

grass   grab   grape

③ This crow gets a ____
from our sprinkler.

_____

drum   dress   drink

④ Every day I fix it a
____ of crumbs.

_____

plate   play   plum

⑤ My crow friend is always
____ to get them.

_____

grade   glad   glass

sc	st	sp	sn	squ
scr	str	sl	sm	sw

1.

2.

3.

4.

5.

6.

7.

8.

9.

10.

11.

12.

Do it this way! Find the word that will finish each sentence. Print it on the line.

1. Did you ever _____ to think about a snake?

2. A _____ has no arms or legs.

3. It has the _____ to get around anyway.

4. It can even _____ and climb.

5. Its _____ looks slimy, but it's dry.

6. Snakes _____ some people, but they are useful.

scare
skin
stop
skill
snake
swim

Now do this! Circle the name of each picture.

1.

swim   stem

2.

scream   screen

3.

smile   smoke

4.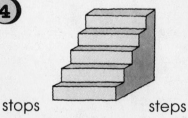

stops   steps

5.

snake   sneak

6.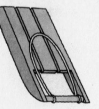

sled   slide

_____

- - - - - - - - - - - - - - - - - -

_____

Give this a try! Circle the answer to each riddle. Print it on the line.

1 All mail needs these.
What are they?

_____

- - - - - - - - - -

_____

stamps   stumps

2 We can ride on it.
What is it?

_____

- - - - - - - - - -

_____

string   swing

3 An elephant has one.
What is it?

_____

- - - - - - - - - -

_____

skunk   trunk

4 We can eat it.
What is it?

_____

- - - - - - - - - -

_____

toast   list

5 It hides your face.
What is it?

_____

- - - - - - - - - -

_____

task   mask

6 We can sleep in it.
What is it?

_____

- - - - - - - - - -

_____

tent   plant

7 We have two of these.
What are they?

_____

- - - - - - - - - -

_____

lands   hands

8 Fish swim in it.
What is it?

_____

- - - - - - - - - -

_____

tank   wink

9 It can float.
What is it?

_____

- - - - - - - - - -

_____

raft   left

Here's what to do! Say the name of each picture. Print its final blend on the line.

1. ring
2. ne
3. sku
4. de
5. sta
6. te
7. tru
8. ra
9. mi

LESSON 41: Final blends

Try this! Find the missing word for each sentence by changing the blend of the word beside the sentence to make a new word. Print it on the line.

1. I went to _____ .   creep

2. I had a strange _____ .   scream

3. The grass changed from green to _____ .   glue

4. The _____ was full of cows saying, "Boo!"   sleet

5. Cotton candy _____ on a tree.   flew

6. A big green _____ went flying past me.   slog

7. I jumped out of bed in a _____ .   crash

8. My _____ had goose bumps.   spin

9. My head was in a _____ .   grin

10. I dumped a _____ of water on top of me.   class

11. That dream really did _____ tricks on me.   clay

Here's what to do! Circle the blend that will complete the word in each sentence. Print the blend on the line.

1 I smile when I climb _____ ees.   tr   fr   br

2 I smile when I _____ im in a pool.   cr   sc   sw

3 I smile when I fish in a _____ eam.   tr   fr   str

4 I smile when I read a _____ ooky book.   sm   tr   sp

5 What makes you _____ ile?   sp   sm   sn

Now do this! Use the blend at the right to make a word that belongs in each sentence. Print it on the line.

1 A _____ frog floated on a lily pad. | gr |

2 The lily pad _____ on a stream. | fl |

3 The _____ flowed through the woods. | str |

4 A black fly flew over the green _____ | fr |

5 The green frog snapped up the _____ fly. | bl |

6 Then it jumped in the stream for a _____ . | sw |

86   **LESSON 42: Test: Consonant blends**

Give this a try! Circle each word with a **Y** that sounds like long **E**.

baby	cry	happy	why
try	every	hurry	tiny
Molly	sandy	shy	puppy
penny	Freddy	funny	bunny
fry	dry	buggy	my
sleepy	sunny	fly	any

Now try this! Circle the words with **Y** that sounds like long **E** in the sentences.

1 Ty and Molly were helping take care of baby Freddy.

2 They heard Freddy cry in his crib.

3 They went to help in a hurry.

4 They had to try everything to make him happy.

5 Ty read him a funny book about fish that fly.

6 Molly said, "You can play with my bunny."

7 Ty made a very silly face.

8 Finally they gave him a ride in his buggy.

9 Then Freddy smiled and wasn't unhappy anymore.

Here's what to do!

Circle each word with a **Y** that sounds like long **I.**

try	Freddy	sly	why	funny
bunny	dry	silly	rocky	my
Ty	windy	by	sky	sunny
fry	fly	happy	muddy	cry
sneaky	lucky	shy	puppy	Molly

Now do this!

Circle the words with **Y** that sounds like long **I** in the sentences.

1. Why do onions make us cry when we are happy?

2. Why is the sky blue on a sunny day?

3. Why do bats fly by night?

4. Why is a desert dry and a swamp muddy?

5. Why can a bird fly but not a puppy?

6. Why do we look silly if we try to fly?

7. Why is a fox sneaky and sly?

8. Why is a bunny shy?

9. Do you ever wonder why?

LESSON 43: The vowel sounds of Y

Try this! Read the word in each paw print. If the **Y** stands for a long **I** sound, color it yellow. If it stands for a long **E** sound, color it orange.

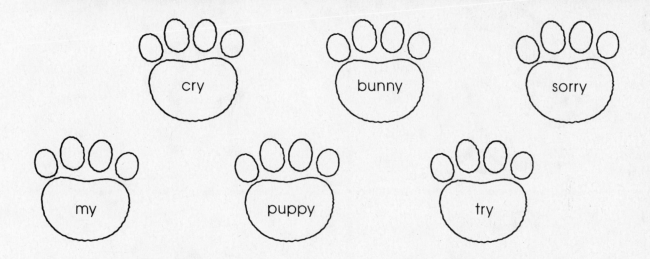

cry

bunny

sorry

my

puppy

try

Now try this! Find a **Y** word from the top of the page that belongs in each sentence. Print it on the line.

1 Yuppy the _____ was digging a hole.

2 Suddenly he heard a _____ from inside.

3 A very angry _____ popped out of the hole.

4 "Why are you digging up _____ happy home?"

5 Yuppy yapped, "Oh, my! I'm very _____ ."

6 "I'll _____ to help you fix it up!"

Here's what to do! Say the name of each picture. Circle each word with the same sound of **Y** as the picture's name.

1
bunny

baby
my
fly
fifty
funny

2
pony

sky
sunny
fairy
cry
Bobby

3
fly

dolly
try
sly
kitty
dry

4
puppy

lady
penny
shy
fry
happy

5
baby

why
silly
lily
by
bunny

6
cry

my
sixty
fly
Sally
sky

7
sky

jelly
Sandy
my
fry
cry

8
candy

lucky
try
fifty
sky
puppy

Do it this way! Circle the word that will finish each sentence.

1. I go to the zoo to see the   chop.   chimp.   check.
2. It smiles to show its   then.   teeth.   there.
3. They are big and   which.   what.   white.
4. It eats bananas by the   bunch.   bench.   beach.
5. Once I saw it eat a   that.   ship.   peach.
6. Sometimes it dumps out its   wish.   dish.   swish.
7. That makes its water   dash.   splash.   wish.
8. Then it takes a nap in the   fresh.   shut.   shade.

Now do this! Find three answer choices from the top of the page that begin with **ch**, **wh**, **th**, and **sh**. Print them on the lines beside the correct consonant digraph.

1.
ch

2.
th

3.
wh

4.
sh

1. Chip and I went to the mall to _____ .
   - ○ chop
   - ○ shop

2. They sell everything _____ .
   - ○ this
   - ○ there

3. We saw so _____ that we wanted.
   - ○ catch
   - ○ much

4. _____ did I want most?
   - ○ What
   - ○ Who

5. Then I saw the model _____ kits.
   - ○ shirt
   - ○ ship

6. _____ was what I wanted most.
   - ○ When
   - ○ This

7. I _____ a clipper ship to make.
   - ○ chose
   - ○ chair

8. _____ chose a spaceship kit.
   - ○ Choose
   - ○ Chip

9. _____ we had lunch.
   - ○ Then
   - ○ That

10. I had a _____ sandwich.
    - ○ cheese
    - ○ chime

11. We almost forgot _____ time it was.
    - ○ that
    - ○ what

12. I kept my ship in good _____ .
    - ○ sharp
    - ○ shape

13. I couldn't wait to _____ my friends.
    - ○ wash
    - ○ show

LESSON 45: Consonant digraphs SH, TH, WH, CH

Give this a try! If the consonant digraph is at the beginning of a word, print the word in the first column. If it is in the middle, print the word in the second. If it is at the end, print the word in the third column.

cheer	quack	thank	stuck	teaching	when
brushing	kicking	peach	dishes	bath	wishing
fish	beach	why	chin	clothing	shell

Beginning	Middle	End

Try this! Say the name of each picture. Circle the consonant digraph you hear.

① th sh ck ch wh

② th sh ck ch wh

③ th sh ck ch wh

④ th sh ck ch wh

⑤ th sh ck ch wh

⑥ th sh ck ch wh

⑦ th sh ck ch wh

⑧ th sh ck ch wh

⑨ th sh ck ch wh

Give this a try! Read each sentence. Find the picture it tells about. Write the sentence letter under the picture.

1

a. John has a knot in the rope.

b. I know what is in the box.

c. Joan turned the knob.

2

a. Theo will knock down the pile.

b. Mom cut it with a knife.

c. Joe knocks on the door.

3

a. The knight wore armor.

b. Tad's knee needs a patch.

c. Grandma likes to knit.

Now try this! Find the answer to each riddle in the box. Print it on the line.

knife	knot	know	knight	knob	knee

1 Something that can cut.

2 Someone who wore armor.

3 Something you can tie.

Here's what to do! Circle the word that will finish each sentence. Print it on the line.

1. I _____ how to do many things.

know   knot

2. I know how to spread butter with a _____ .

knot   knife

3. I know how to touch my _____ to my chin.

knees   knew

4. I know how to tie _____ .

knots   knits

5. I know how to turn a door _____ .

knee   knob

6. I know how to read about _____ .

know   knights

7. I know you _____ how to do many things, too.

knit   know

Now do this! Think of a word that begins with **kn** and rhymes with each word. Print it on the line.

1. snow

2. block

3. wife

4. blew

5. see

6. hot

Here's what to do!

Find the name of each picture in the box. Print it on the line.

apple	eagle	people
candle	buckle	whistle
turtle	bottle	table

1

2

3

4

5

6

7

8

9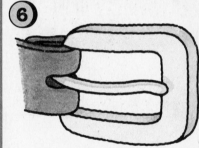

LESSON 48: Words ending in LE

97

Do it this way! Find the word that will finish each sentence. Print it on the line.

1. A _____ has its own shell for a safe house.

2. It can swim in a _____ .

3. It can climb on rocks and _____ .

4. An _____ might fly over and scare it.

5. Then the turtle can _____ safely in its shell.

pebbles

eagle

turtle

huddle

puddle

---

1. I have a _____ pet turtle.

2. It looks a little like a small green _____ .

3. When I hold it, its feet wiggle and _____ my hand.

4. Then I laugh and _____ .

5. I named my turtle _____ .

giggle

little

Wiggle

pickle

tickle

_____

_____

Give this a try! Find the word that will finish each sentence.
Print it on the line.

wrap

wren

write

1 To move around is to _____ .

2 The opposite of right is _____ .

3 A small bird is a _____ .

4 A thing that is ruined is a _____ .

5 To hide a gift in paper is to _____ .

6 When you put a story on paper you _____ .

7 Your _____ holds your hand to your arm.

8 A truck that clears away wrecks is a _____ .

9 A tool that helps us twist is a _____ .

wren

wreck

wrap

write

wrist

wrench

wrecker

wrong

wriggle

LESSON 49: Consonant digraph WR

99

wren	wrecker	wrap	wrist
wrench	wreath	writer	typewriter

1 I am round and pretty.
You can hang me up.
What am I?

_____

2 I hide a gift.
You tear me up.
What am I?

_____

3 I can fly.
I like to sing.
What is my name?

_____

4 I am a useful tool.
I can fix things.
What is my name?

_____

5 I am next to a hand.
I can twist and bend.
What am I called?

_____

6 I can print.
People press my keys.
What is my name?

_____

7 I am a big truck.
I tow things away.
What am I called?

_____

8 I write stories.
They can be real or make believe.
What am I called?

_____

Do it this way! Find the word that will finish each sentence in the box. Print it on the line.

knows	wrong	Knights	write
wrapped	written	knees	knew

1. I like to read stories _____ about knights.

2. _____ lived a long time ago.

3. They _____ themselves in metal armor.

4. It was the only way they _____ to protect themselves.

5. The armor needed to bend at the wrists,

   elbows, and _____ .

6. No one _____ how they could do much in all that armor.

7. I wonder if anything ever went _____ with armor.

8. I'll find out all I can and _____ a report about it.

LESSON 50: Reviewing consonant digraphs KN, WR   101

Try this! Say the name of each picture. Print the consonant digraphs where you hear them in the words. Some words will have two consonant digraphs.

① ____ ___ ___

② ____ ___ ___

③ ____ ___ ___

④ ____ ___ ___

⑤ ____ ___ ___

⑥ ____ ___ ___

⑦ ____ ___ ___

⑧ ____ ___ ___

⑨ ____ ___ ___

LESSON 50: Reviewing consonant digraphs SH, TH, WH, CH, CK, KN, WR

Give this a try! Find the answer to each riddle. Print its letter on the line.

1 A bike rolls on them. _____ **a.** sheep

2 It gives us wool. _____ **b.** brush

3 It is something we use for our hair. _____ **c.** whale

4 It can blow water from its head. _____ **d.** wheels

5 It is not fair to do this. _____ **a.** teeth

6 This is a chair fit for a king. _____ **b.** rattle

7 These show when we smile. _____ **c.** cheat

8 Wind makes a door do this. _____ **d.** throne

9 These are fun to find on the beach. _____ **a.** peaches

10 These taste good. _____ **b.** shells

11 Smoke goes up this. _____ **c.** clock

12 This tells us the time. _____ **d.** chimney

Now try this! Say the name of each picture. Print its missing letters on the line.

1. eese

2. ell

3. app

4. ock

5. ite

6. tru

7. di es

8. cand

9. eel

LESSON 51: Test: Consonant digraphs; ending LE

_____

_____

Here's what to do! Find the word that will finish each sentence. Print it on the line.

barn   star   car

(1) I picked out a new model _____ kit.

(2) I got two _____ of paint, too.

(3) I could hardly wait to _____ on it.

(4) I fit the _____ together.

(5) The tires were _____ to fit, but I did it.

(6) I glued it so it wouldn't fall _____

(7) I stuck gold _____ stickers on the sides.

(8) The best _____ was showing it to my friends.

apart

star

hard

part

car

start

parts

jars

LESSON 52: The sound of AR   105

_____

Do it this way! Finish each sentence. Use a word that rhymes with the word beside each sentence. Print it on the line.

_____

1 A _____ is a very interesting animal.

bark

2 Its teeth are very _____ .

carp

3 It has no problem tearing food _____ .

start

4 Sharks can grow to be very _____ .

barge

5 I live _____ from the ocean where sharks live.

star

6 I am lucky to live near an animal _____ .

lark

7 I can watch sharks there free from _____ .

farm

Now do this! Print two rhyming words under each word.

1 mark

2 start

3 hard

Here's what to do! Read each riddle. Answer it with a word that rhymes with the word beside the riddle. Print it on the line.

Mark and Lori like to play word games. Do you think words are fun?

1. Something to pop and eat. _____ | horn |

2. Something on a unicorn. _____ | born |

3. Something we eat with. _____ | cork |

4. Something with rain, wind, and thunder. _____ | form |

5. Something we can play or watch. _____ | port |

6. Something on a rose. _____ | born |

7. Something beside the sea. _____ | tore |

8. Something to stop up a bottle. _____ | pork |

(1)

home
horse
horn

(2)

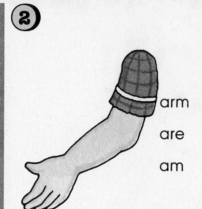

arm
are
am

(3)

barn
bark
book

(4)

home
horse
horn

(5)

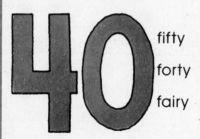

fifty
forty
fairy

(6)

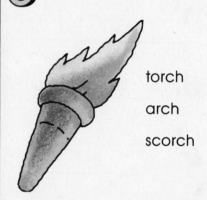

torch
arch
scorch

(7)

car
card
cost

(8)

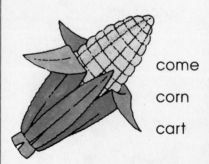

come
corn
cart

(9)

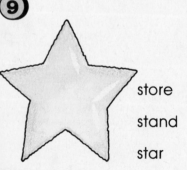

store
stand
star

Give this a try! Circle each word with the same sound as the name of the picture.

① ir

first
fork
skirt
shirt
girl

bird

② ur

curb
purse
card
nurse
fur

turtle

③ er

batter
letter
hammer
park
clerk

fern

Now try this! Find the name of each picture in the words above. Print the names on the lines.

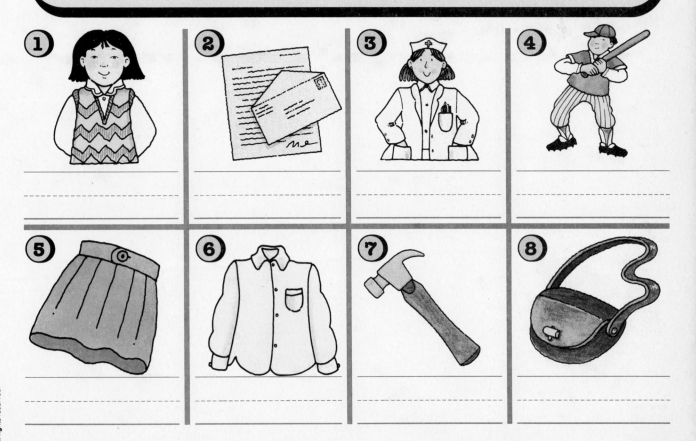

①	②	③	④

⑤	⑥	⑦	⑧

Do it this way! Circle the name of each picture. Color the box with the same vowel with **r**.

1
bird
barn
burn

er	or	ir

2
first
batter
farm

ir	er	ar

3
tar
turtle
third

ur	ar	or

4
hammer
farmer
summer

ir	or	er

5
shirt
skirt
scarf

ar	ir	ur

6
goat
garden
girl

ir	or	ur

Now do this! Circle the word that will finish each sentence. Print it on the line.

1 Cats have _____ and purr.

far
fur
first

2 Birds have feathers and _____ .

chip
cheat
chirp

3 _____ have very hard shells.

Birds
Turtles
Ferns

4 Have you _____ wondered why?

clever
ever
winner

Here's what to do! Find the vowel followed by **r** in each word. Print the two letters on the line. Print the number of the picture with the same two letters.

① car ② horn ③ bird ④ hammer ⑤ turtle

① part

② verse

③ turn

④ pork

⑤ first

⑥ party

⑦ third

⑧ bark

⑨ fern

⑩ storm

⑪ her

⑫ chirp

⑬ park

⑭ horse

⑮ fur

⑯ skirt

⑰ curb

⑱ short

LESSON 55: Reviewing AR, OR, IR, ER, UR 111

1 Many different things happen in sp__ts.　　　　er　or　ir

2 A diver jumps into the water head f__st.　　　　ur　ir　ar

3 A s__fer stands up on the ocean waves.　　　　ar　or　ur

4 A ski jump__ hops off high cliffs.　　　　ir　er　ur

5 There __e some sports I like to play.　　　　or　er　ar

6 There are oth__s I'd rather watch.　　　　ar　ir　er

bark	skirt	car	park	fur	corn

1 It is part of a dress.

2 You like to eat it.

3 Dogs do this.

4 A rabbit has it.

5 A person can drive it.

6 We play games in it.

Here's what to do! Say the name of each picture. Fill in the bubble beside its vowel with **r.**

1. ○ ur ○ or ○ ar

2. ○ ar ○ er ○ or

3. ○ ar ○ er ○ or

4. ○ er ○ or ○ ar

5. ○ ar ○ er ○ or

6. ○ or ○ ar ○ ir

7. ○ ar ○ or ○ ir

8. ○ or ○ ur ○ ar

9. ○ ir ○ or ○ ar

LESSON 56: Reviewing AR, OR, IR, ER, UR

113

Here's what to do! Do what the sentences tell you to do. Draw a line under each word with **ar**, **or**, **ir**, **er**, or **ur**.

1. Do you see the skirt? Circle the skirt. Color the skirt purple.

2. See the letter. Color it green. Make a black dot near it.

3. Can you see the fern? Color it green. Draw a line under it.

4. Find the turkey. Color its feathers orange and yellow.

5. See the barn. Make a little black **X** under it. Color the barn red.

6. Do you see the corn? Color the corn yellow. Draw a box around the corn.

7. See the star. Color it blue. Make two red dots near the star.

8. Look at the turtle. Make a blue **X** under it. Color it green and black.

_____

- -

_____

D̲o it this way! Print one word that means the same as the two words beside each line.

she will　　　　**she'll**

The short way to write **she will** is **she'll**.

you'll	they'll	she'll	we'll	I'll	he'll

1 I will _____

2 he will _____

3 we will _____

4 they will _____

5 she will _____

6 you will _____

N̲ow do this! Print the short form of the two underlined words in each sentence.

1 I <u>will</u> get in the boat and you'll get in, too. _____

2 <u>He will</u> climb aboard. _____

3 <u>She will</u> join us and jump in. _____

4 <u>They will</u> hop in for the ride. _____

5 All aboard? Oh, no! <u>We will</u> sink! _____

Give this a try! Print each word that means the same as the two words beside each line.

can not   **can't**

The short way to write **can not** is **can't.**

can't	couldn't	weren't	don't
didn't	aren't	isn't	won't

1 are not _____

2 do not _____

3 did not _____

4 will not _____

5 were not _____

6 is not _____

7 could not _____

8 can not _____

Now try this! Print two words that mean the same as each underlined word.

1 Mitten the kitten <u>can't</u> get down from the tree.

_____

2 She <u>isn't</u> brave enough to climb down.

_____

3 We <u>haven't</u> any problem getting her down.

_____

4 "<u>Aren't</u> you a lucky kitten to have friends to help?"

_____

Do it this way! Circle two words in each sentence that can be made into one of the contractions in the box. Print the contraction on the line.

he is = he's	That is = That's
she is = she's	It is = It's

1

It is Rocky's birthday.

_____

2

What a surprise he is going to get!

_____

3

Jess has his gift, but she is hiding it.

_____

4

Do you know what Rocky will get? Look at the picture at the top. That is what Rocky wants the most.

_____

You have = You've   I have = I've

We have = We've   They have = They've

1

I have made you smile.

_____

_ _ _ _ _ _ _ _ _ _ _ _ _ _ _ _ _ _ _ _

_____ made you smile.

2

We have shown you tricks.

_____

_ _ _ _ _ _ _ _ _ _ _ _ _ _ _ _ _ _ _ _

_____ shown you tricks.

3

They have tossed a ball with their noses.

_____

_ _ _ _ _ _ _ _ _ _ _ _ _ _ _ _ _ _ _ _

_____ tossed a ball with their noses.

4

You have had a good time.

_____

_ _ _ _ _ _ _ _ _ _ _ _ _ _ _ _ _ _ _ _

_____ had a good time.

Give this a try!

Print two words that mean the same as the underlined word in each sentence.

1. <u>Let's</u> have a party.

2. <u>We'll</u> ask our friends to come.

3. <u>I'm</u> going to pop popcorn.

4. <u>They're</u> going to bring games.

5. <u>We're</u> going to have fun!

Now try this!

Print the contraction that means the same as the two words beside the line.

1. you are

2. she is

3. I am

4. it is

5. let us

6. they are

7. we are

8. we will

9. he is

10. they will

Here's what to do! Print the letter of each contraction next to the words that have the same meaning.

a. we're	**b.** you'll	**c.** it's	**d.** can't
e. I'm	**f.** he's	**g.** won't	**h.** let's
i. don't	**j.** she's	**k.** you're	**l.** isn't
m. she'll	**n.** we'll	**o.** I'll	**p.** I've

1 _____ I am **2** _____ we are **3** _____ will not **4** _____ he is

5 _____ you will **6** _____ let us **7** _____ can not **8** _____ it is

9 _____ is not **10** _____ you are **11** _____ I will **12** _____ we will

13 _____ do not **14** _____ I have **15** _____ she will **16** _____ she is

Now do this! Circle the missing word for each sentence. Print it on the line.

1 _____ go skating in the park. _____

Let's
I'm
It's

2 _____ help you find your skates. _____

I'm
I'll
I've

3 I think _____ going to have fun. _____

won't
we've
we're

Give this a try! Print two words that mean the same as each contraction.

① I've _____

② didn't _____

③ he'll _____

④ you've _____

⑤ they're _____

⑥ let's _____

⑦ isn't _____

⑧ won't _____

⑨ hasn't _____

⑩ I'll _____

Now try this! Print the contraction for the underlined words in each sentence.

① <u>He will</u> read his story to the class. _____

② <u>Let us</u> listen to him. _____

③ <u>You are</u> a good reader, Jake. _____

④ <u>Will</u> you <u>not</u> read your story again? _____

⑤ <u>I will</u> help you make a book from your story. _____

Do it this way! Print the contraction for the two words beside each line.

1 I have _____

2 can not _____

3 do not _____

4 could not _____

5 let us _____

6 there is _____

7 did not _____

8 you have _____

Now do this! Circle the missing contraction for each sentence. Print it on the line.

1 _____ a surprise for Linda. _____ Didn't   It's

2 _____ her new bike. _____ That's   Isn't

3 She _____ guess what it is. _____ won't   you're

4 She _____ think she'll get one. _____ aren't   doesn't

5 _____ here now! _____ She's   You'll

6 "Linda, _____ going to show you something!" _____ we're   don't

_____

- -

_____

Here's what to do! Circle the word that will finish each sentence. Print it on the line. Color one or two pictures in each box to match the answer.

If a word ends in **x, z, ss, sh,** or **ch,** usually add **es** to make it mean more than one.

1 At the zoo we saw some

seal   seals

_____

_ _ _ _ _ _ _ _ _ _ _ _ _ _ _ _ _

_____ .

2 We like to eat fresh

peach   peaches

_____

_ _ _ _ _ _ _ _ _ _ _ _ _ _ _ _ _

_____ .

3 We have toys in two

box   boxes

_____

_ _ _ _ _ _ _ _ _ _ _ _ _ _ _ _ _

_____ .

4 June will use a hair

brush   brushes

_____

_ _ _ _ _ _ _ _ _ _ _ _ _ _ _ _ _

_____ .

5 Zack's mother gave him a

cap   caps

_____

_ _ _ _ _ _ _ _ _ _ _ _ _ _ _ _ _

_____ .

6 Just look at those

dog   dogs

_____

_ _ _ _ _ _ _ _ _ _ _ _ _ _ _ _ _

_____ .

7 Look at those shiny

star   stars

_____

_ _ _ _ _ _ _ _ _ _ _ _ _ _ _ _ _

_____ !

8 The box was used for

mitten   mittens

_____

_ _ _ _ _ _ _ _ _ _ _ _ _ _ _ _ _

_____ .

LESSON 61: Plural endings -S, -ES

123

Here's what to do! Read each shopping list. Finish each word by adding the ending **s** or **es**. Print it on the line.

Steve's List

1. 2 book _____ to read
2. 3 paint brush _____
3. 6 red pencil _____
4. 2 jar _____ of paste

Peggy's List

1. 5 block _____
2. 2 box _____ of clay
3. 3 top _____ to spin
4. 2 puzzle _____

Pam's List

1. 8 dish _____
2. 8 cup _____
3. 4 glass _____
4. 2 patch _____ for jeans

Ron's List

1. 7 apple _____
2. 5 peach _____
3. 4 sandwich _____
4. 2 bunch _____ of grapes

LESSON 61: Plural endings -S, -ES

Give this a try!

Add **ing** to each base word. Print the new word on the line.

1 sleep _____

2 jump _____

3 play _____

4 help _____

5 start _____

6 work _____

7 fish _____

8 turn _____

Now try this!

Add **ing** to the word beside each sentence. Print it on the line.

1 We are _____ for the bus. | wait |

2 Doris and Mark are _____ rope. | jump |

3 Sam is _____ for the bus. | look |

4 Bart's dog is _____ with him. | stay |

5 Terry is _____ his lunch. | hold |

6 Now the bus is _____ our corner! | turn |

LESSON 62: Inflectional ending -ING   125

Do it this way! Add **ed** to each base word. Print the new word on the line. Use the new words to finish the sentences.

1 look

2 want

3 help

4 leap

5 fix

6 ask

---

1 Jess and I _____ to catch a frog for a pet.

2 We _____ everywhere for frogs.

3 Suddenly a frog _____ over a rock.

4 We _____ it a box for a frog home.

Now try this! Print each base word on the line.

1 locked

2 marched

3 dreamed

4 played

5 cleaned

6 passed

Give this a try! Add **es** or **ed** to the base word to finish each sentence.

1 The girls play _____ baseball after school.

2 Randy always watches and wish _____ for Jean's team to win.

3 The ball comes fast and brush _____ past Jean's bat. Strike one!

4 The pitcher throws and the ball buzz _____ toward the plate.

5 Jean swings as the ball pass _____ by.

6 This time Jean has not miss _____ .

7 Randy cheer _____ until he was hoarse.

Now try this! Add **s** or **es** to each base word. Print the new word on the line.

see	fox	bush	patch	mail	line

_____   _____

_____   _____

_____   _____

_____   _____

LESSON 63: Reviewing endings -S, -ES, -ED

127

Here's what to do! Circle the word that will finish each sentence. Print it on the line.

1 Dad goes _____ in the stream in the woods.

fishing
fished
fishes

2 While the time _____ , he looks around.

passed
passing
passes

3 Yesterday some quacking ducks _____ by.

floating
floats
floated

4 Frogs were _____ in and out of the water.

jumped
jumping
jumps

5 Some birds were _____ each other.

helped
helps
helping

6 While one _____ the nest, the other looked for food.

watched
watching
watches

7 They _____ to feed their hungry babies.

needs
needed
needing

8 Dad _____ looking around as much as he likes fishing.

liking
likes
like

_____

- - - - - - - - - - - - - - - -

_____

Do it this way! Add **ing** to the base word in the box. Print it on the line.

When a short-vowel word ends in a single consonant, usually double the consonant before adding **ing**.

_____
- -
1 Maria and Jess were _____ to go shopping.

| plan |

- -
2 First they went _____ in the park.

| jog |

- -
3 Children were _____ on the swings.

| swing |

_____
- -
4 Some horseback riders were _____ around.

| trot |

_____
- -
5 They saw two bunnies _____ by.

| hop |

_____
- -
6 A turtle was _____ at a bug.

| snap |

_____
- -
7 A man was _____ hot dogs.

| roast |

_____
- -
8 His dog was _____ for one.

| beg |

- -
9 "_____ in the park was fun," said Maria.

| Run |

_____
- -
10 "Now let's go _____ ," Jess said.

| shop |

LESSON 64: Inflectional ending -ING; doubling the final consonant **129**

Here's what to do! Add **ed** to the word beside each sentence. Print it on the line.

When a short-vowel word ends in a single consonant, usually double the consonant before adding **ed**.

1) Wags _____ up on me with a happy smile.

hop

2) When I _____ him my hand got muddy.

pat

3) "Wags, you need to be _____ !"

scrub

4) I _____ him up and dipped him in the tub.

pick

5) He _____ around and sloshed water everywhere.

jump

6) When I _____ , Wags was clean but I was a mess!

stop

Now do this! Add **ed** and **ing** to each word. Print the new words on the lines.

1) wag

2) clean

3) hop

Here's what to do!

Add **ing** or **ed** to each base word. Print the new word on the line.

If a word ends with a silent **e**, drop the **e** before adding **ing** or **ed**.

ing

ed

1 hope _____

2 get _____

3 eat _____

4 dive _____

5 save _____

6 camp _____

7 sit _____

8 bat _____

9 hike _____

10 close _____

11 joke _____

12 bake _____

13 smile _____

14 skate _____

15 rub _____

16 pass _____

17 help _____

18 trim _____

LESSON 65: Inflectional endings -ING and -ED; dropping final E

Give this a try! Add **ing** to each base word. Print the new word on the line.

1 ride _____

2 fry _____

3 rub _____

4 hide _____

5 frame _____

6 dig _____

7 take _____

8 jump _____

9 poke _____

10 whip _____

Now try this! Add **ed** to each base word. Print the new word on the line.

1 pin _____

2 rock _____

3 chase _____

4 hop _____

5 march _____

6 bake _____

7 wish _____

8 drop _____

9 hope _____

10 quack _____

LESSON 65: Inflectional endings -ING and -ED

Do it this way! Add the ending in the box to each word below it. Print the new word on the line.

ing	ed	s or es
① wave	**④** skip	**⑦** peach
② drop	**⑤** like	**⑧** pass
③ smile	**⑥** press	**⑨** tree

Now do this! Finish each sentence by adding the correct ending to the base word. Print the new word on the line.

① I like _____ all kinds of books. `read`

② I _____ a good story book at the library. `spot`

③ I _____ a pie after I read a cook book. `bake`

④ My brother is _____ his money to buy books. `save`

⑤ He _____ every joke book he can find. `get`

Do it this way! Add **ed** or **ing** to the words in the box. Use the new words to finish the sentences.

bake	cut	have
plan	smile	make

1. We are _____ dinner for our grandparents.

2. We are _____ to have pizza and salad.

3. Sal is _____ vegetables for the salad.

4. Bernie _____ dessert.

5. We're _____ fun!

Now do this! Draw a box around each base word.

1. dressed
2. buzzes
3. cooked
4. plays
5. puffed
6. brushing
7. drives
8. loading
9. boxes
10. dishes
11. snapping
12. parking
13. wished
14. stayed
15. swimming

_____

_____

_____

Give this a try! Add the ending **ful** to each base word. Use the new words to finish the sentences.

hopeful
The ending is **ful**.
The base word is **hope**.

1 care

_____

2 cheer

_____

3 wonder

_____

4 use

_____

1 Pablo thought a skateboard would be very _____ .

2 He promised to be _____ if he got one.

3 His family looked _____ when they gave him his gift.

4 It was a skateboard! How _____ !

Now try this! Draw a box around each base word.

1 u s e f u l   **2** h o p e f u l   **3** r e s t f u l   **4** g r a t e f u l

5 t h a n k f u l   **6** c h e e r f u l   **7** p l a y f u l   **8** c a r e f u l

Do it this way! Add **less** or **ness** to each word. Print the new word on the line. Use the new words to finish the sentences.

less

1 use _____

2 sleep _____

3 harm _____

4 fear _____

ness

5 thick _____

6 dark _____

7 loud _____

8 sharp _____

1 It is _____ to tell me the bear is harmless.

2 I am not _____ .

3 Its eyes are glowing in the _____ .

4 The _____ of its snarls worries me.

5 I can almost feel the _____ of its teeth.

6 I see the _____ of its strong legs.

7 It is only _____ when its in the cage!

LESSON 67: Adding suffixes -LESS, -NESS

Here's what to do! Add the ending **ly** to each base word. Print the new word on the line.

quickly   The bunny runs quickly.

The ending is **ly**.
The base word is **quick**.

(1) glad _____

(2) swift _____

(3) soft _____

(4) brave _____

(5) loud _____

(6) slow _____

Now do this! Circle each **ly** ending in the sentences. Print the base words on the lines.

(1) Tigers walk softly. _____

(2) Lions roar loudly. _____

(3) Turtles crawl slowly. _____

(4) Deer run swiftly. _____

(5) I watch them at the zoo gladly. _____

1

_____ quick   **a.** slowly

_____ sweet   **b.** quickly

_____ slow   **c.** sweetly

_____ loud   **d.** loudly

2

_____ glad   **a.** softly

_____ soft   **b.** nearly

_____ near   **c.** lovely

_____ love   **d.** gladly

3

_____ use   **a.** playful

_____ play   **b.** handful

_____ cheer   **c.** useful

_____ hand   **d.** cheerful

4

_____ care   **a.** fearless

_____ sleeve   **b.** jobless

_____ fear   **c.** careless

_____ job   **d.** sleeveless

5

_____ home   **a.** cheerless

_____ use   **b.** homeless

_____ wire   **c.** useless

_____ cheer   **d.** wireless

6

_____ good   **a.** softness

_____ dark   **b.** sadness

_____ sad   **c.** darkness

_____ soft   **d.** goodness

Here's what to do! Add an ending from the box to finish the word in each sentence. Print it on the line.

ly	ful	less	ness

1. Polly was usually brave and fear _____ .

2. Today she was lone _____ in her new school.

3. She thought of her old friends with sad _____ .

4. Sudden _____ she saw some girls smiling at her.

5. Now she felt more cheer _____ .

Now do this! Read the words in the box. Print each word below its definition.

fearless	darkness	safely	playful

1. with no fear

2. full of play

3. in a safe way

4. being dark

Do it this way! Add the ending in each box to the base words. Print the new words on the lines.

ly

1. quiet _____

2. glad _____

ful

5. use _____

6. skill _____

less

3. help _____

4. fear _____

ness

7. dark _____

8. black _____

Now do this! Add an ending to the base word to finish each sentence.

1. Owls like the _____ of night. | dark |

2. Their sharp eyes are very _____ | use |

3. They are _____ hunters. | skill |

4. They fly _____ with no sound. | quiet |

5. After a long night, owls _____ nap all day. | glad |

Here's what to do! Add the endings **er** and **est** to each word. Print the new words on the lines.

		er	est
1	near		
2	long		
3	fast		
4	dark		
5	thick		
6	deep		
7	soft		
8	clean		

Now do this! Draw a picture to show the meaning of each word.

1

2

3

long

longer

longest

Give this a try! Finish each sentence by adding **er** or **est** to each base word. Use **er** to tell about two things. Use **est** to tell about more than two things.

(1)

Meg is tall_____ than Jay.

(2)

The rock is hard_____ than the soap.

(3)

The horse is the fast_____ of the three.

(4)

The top fish is the long_____ .

(5)

Ice is cold_____ than water.

Give this a try! Add **er** and **est** to each word. Print the new words on the lines.

When a word ends in **y** after a consonant, change the **y** to **i** before adding **er** or **est**.

er	est
1 silly		
2 happy		
3 windy		
4 fluffy		

Now try this! Finish each sentence by adding **er** or **est** to the base word in the box.

1 Today was Justin's _____ kind of day.   happy

2 The bus ride to school was _____ than usual.   bumpy

3 It was _____ than it had been all week.   sunny

4 He made up the _____ joke he could.   silly

5 The other kids said it was the _____ one they had heard.   funny

LESSON 71: Suffixes -ER, -EST; words ending in Y

Give this a try! Circle the name of each picture.

When a word ends in **y** after a consonant, change the **y** to **i** before adding **es**.

1 daisy   daisies

 2
cherry   cherries

 3
lily   lilies

Now try this! Use the rule to add **es** to the word beside each sentence. Finish the sentence by printing the new word on the line.

1 Today we all wrote _____ for our class book. | story

2 Mine was about my dog's new _____ . | puppy

3 Lily wrote about planting a garden of _____ . | daisy

4 Penny's story was about raising _____ . | bunny

5 Marty gave ideas for birthday _____ | party

6 Jerry told how to take care of _____ . | pony

7 Tony wrote about his collection of _____ . | penny

8 When we finished, we made extra _____ . | copy

Do it this way! Add endings to make the words mean more than one.

1 bunny _____

2 city _____

3 box _____

4 lily _____

5 dress _____

6 pony _____

Now do this! Circle the word that will finish each sentence. Print it on the line. Then print the name of each picture.

1 Mary's birthday (party,   parties) was fun. _____

2 Her dad read scary (story,   stories) in the dark. _____

3 We tried to toss (penny,   pennies) into bottles. _____

4 Instead of cake, we ate (cherry,   cherries) pie.

1 _____

2 _____

3 _____

LESSON 72: Suffix -ES; words ending in Y   145

Here's what to do! Change the **y** to **i** and add **es** to the word in each box. Print the new words to finish the sentences.

1. Farms are different from _____ . `city`

2. Sometimes my friends and our _____ visit a farm. `family`

3. We like to ride the _____ . `pony`

4. There are many different animal _____ . `baby`

5. It's fun to play with the _____ . `bunny`

6. We almost always get to see some _____ . `puppy`

7. Fruits and _____ grow on farms. `berry`

8. Sometimes we climb trees to pick _____ . `cherry`

9. I like to write _____ about our trips to the country. `story`

Do it this way!

Find the word in the box that names each picture. Print it on the line.

sail	pay	rain
tail	hay	tray
spray	chain	nail

1

2

3

4

5

6

7

8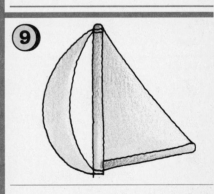

9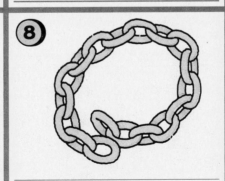

Here's what to do! Find the word in the box that answers each riddle. Print it on the line.

chain	stain	mailbox	hay
pail	rain	hair	paint
chair	train	gray	sail

1 I ride on railroad tracks.

2 You drop letters in me.

3 I am a blend of black and white.

4 If I start, you put on a raincoat.

5 You can sit on me.

6 I am made of many links.

7 I am part of a boat.

8 I am an ink spot on a shirt.

9 I am piled in a stack.

10 I am used with a brush.

Do it this way! Circle the name of each picture.

1. sell
   seal
   seed

2. jeep
   jeans
   peep

3. bean
   bed
   bee

4. leaf
   lean
   leak

5. jeeps
   jeans
   jets

6. feed
   feet
   feel

7. deep
   deeds
   deer

8. meat
   met
   team

9. eat
   each
   ear

eager	seem	meal	feet
beaver	each	teeth	leaves

1. A _____ likes to chew down trees. _____

2. It makes a _____ of the bark. _____

3. It drags _____ branch home to build a dam. _____

4. It only _____ the stump behind. _____

5. A beaver's _____ have to be strong. _____

6. Its webbed _____ help it swim along. _____

7. Beavers always _____ to be working. _____

8. That is why busy people are called "_____ beavers." _____

1

Jack used a _____
to dig up the soil.

hay
hoe
hot

2

Ted wore a white shirt

and a red _____ .

tie
toe
lie

3

The _____ ate the grass
on the slope.

die
doe
day

4

Penny put her _____
in the cold lake.

tie
top
toe

5

Grandma baked a _____
with fresh peaches.

pie
pine
pile

6

_____ can pay for a shirt
with his name on it.

Jog
Joe
Jet

LESSON 75: Regular double vowels IE, OE

Give this a try! Print the name for each picture on the line below it.

| boat | rainbow | goat | bow | soap | bowl |

1
_____

2
_____

3
_____

4
_____

5
_____

6
_____

Now try this! Circle the word that will finish each sentence. Print it on the line.

1 Isn't it fun to ride in a _____ ?   _____   boot   boat

2 Sailboats move when the wind _____ .   _____   blows   blues

3 Pull on the oars to _____ a boat.   _____   raw   row

4 Tugboats _____ other boats along.   _____   tow   too

Do it this way! Print the letter of each missing word on the line.

1. Farmer Gray shears his _____ .

2. He _____ weeds in the garden.

3. Farmer Gray picks a ripe _____ for a snack.

4. He will pick a few more to make a _____ .

5. Then it is time to _____ the shed.

6. He is ready to sleep at the end of the _____ .

| a. day |
| b. paint |
| c. peach |
| d. pie |
| e. sheep |
| f. hoes |

Now do this! Make a word to answer each riddle by adding beginning and ending consonants.

1. It is something to put on.   _____ oa _____

2. A dog wags it.   _____ ai _____

3. They need socks.   _____ ee _____

4. Seven of them make a week.   _____ ay _____

LESSON 76: Reviewing regular double vowels AI, AY, EE, EA, OA, IE, OE

| note | pie | hay | tree | jeans | boat | feet | daisy |

Now do this! Find the double vowel that will finish the word in
each sentence. Print it on the line.

(1) Joe had a very bad d _____ .

(2) The hose sprang a l _____ k.

(3) He got s _____ ked.

(4) Have you ever had a day like J _____ ?

ai

ay

ee

ea

oa

ie

oe

Here's what to do! Circle the word that will finish each
sentence. Print it on the line.

1 I felt something ____ in my mouth.

broom
loose
room

2 Was it a ____ ?

tool
moon
tooth

3 I ran to my ____ .

room
zoo
boom

4 I stood on a ____ to look in the mirror.

spoon
stool
pool

5 My tooth might fall out ____ .

moon
soon
spoon

6 At ____ it was time for lunch.

soon
cool
noon

7 I took a bite of ____ with my spoon.

food
fool
shoot

8 Out came my loose tooth on the ____ .

soothe
tooth
spoon

9 My friend lost a tooth, ____ .

too
zoo
tool

Here's what to do! Circle the word that will finish each sentence. Print it on the line.

1 I was looking for a good _____ .

look   shook   book

2 I took a _____ at a cook book.

wood   hood   look

3 I _____ in line to pay for my book.

good   took   stood

4 I tried a _____ recipe.

hook   took   cookie

5 The cookies were very _____ .

look   good   shook

Now do this! Print the missing letters of each picture's name. Print the missing letters for a word that rhymes with it.

1   **2**   **3**   **4**

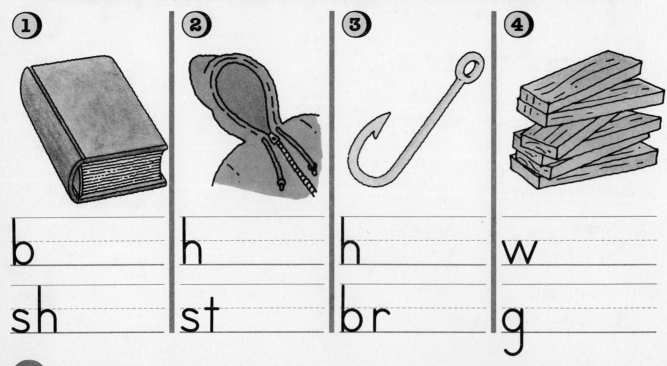

b
sh

h
st

h
br

w
g

Here's what to do! Find the word that will finish each sentence. Print it on the line.

1 Good morning!
Take a deep
_____ .

2 It will clear your
_____ .

3 Are you ready for
_____ ?

4 Breakfast is
_____ for you.

5 Here is _____
for toast.

6 You can _____
butter and jam
on it.

| breakfast |
| ready |
| spread |
| bread |
| breath |
| head |

Now do this! Circle the correct word to finish each sentence.

1 What is the (feather, weather, leather) like today?

2 Will you need to wear a (sweater, weather, meadow) ?

3 Maybe you will need a (ready, heavy, cleanser) coat.

4 Is it cold enough for (bread, thread, leather) boots?

5 Cover your (head, heavy, breakfast) with a warm hat.

6 Now you are (meadow, heavy, ready) to go outside.

LESSON 78: Vowel digraph EA   **157**

Do it this way! Say the name of each picture. Circle the words with the same **ea** sound as the picture's name.

1

seat
bread
meat
bean

2

bread
beach
heavy
treat

3
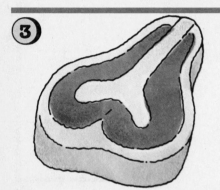

reach
steam
break
great

4

dream
mean
beak
health

5

head
heavy
lean
steak

6

steak
tea
teacher
great

7

beaver
team
leather
beans

8

bread
weather
seal
leather

Here's what to do!
Find the word that will finish each sentence. Print it on the line.

saw	August	paw

1. _____ is a lazy month.

2. _____ and I play games in the shade.

3. We _____ the picnic basket to the lake.

4. After swimming, we _____ and nap in the sun.

5. We sip lemonade through _____ .

6. My baby brother _____ on the beach.

7. Summer's end is _____ near.

8. Soon _____ will come and school will start.

drawing
autumn
straws
haul
August
yawn
crawls
Paula

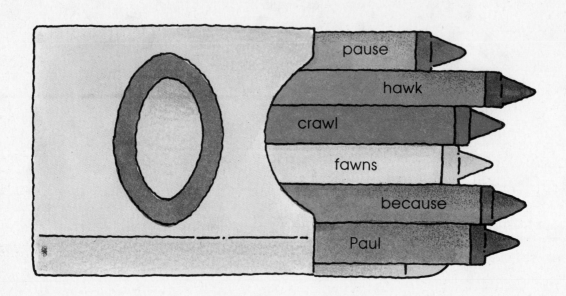

pause
hawk
crawl
fawns
because
Paul

(1) _____ likes to draw.

(2) He draws and draws without a _____ .

(3) He can make a _____ with sharp claws.

(4) His turtles really seem to _____ .

(5) He draws _____ hiding in trees.

(6) Why does Paul draw so much? Just _____ .

Here's what to do!
Say the name of the first picture in each row. Fill in the bubble below the picture with the same vowel sound.

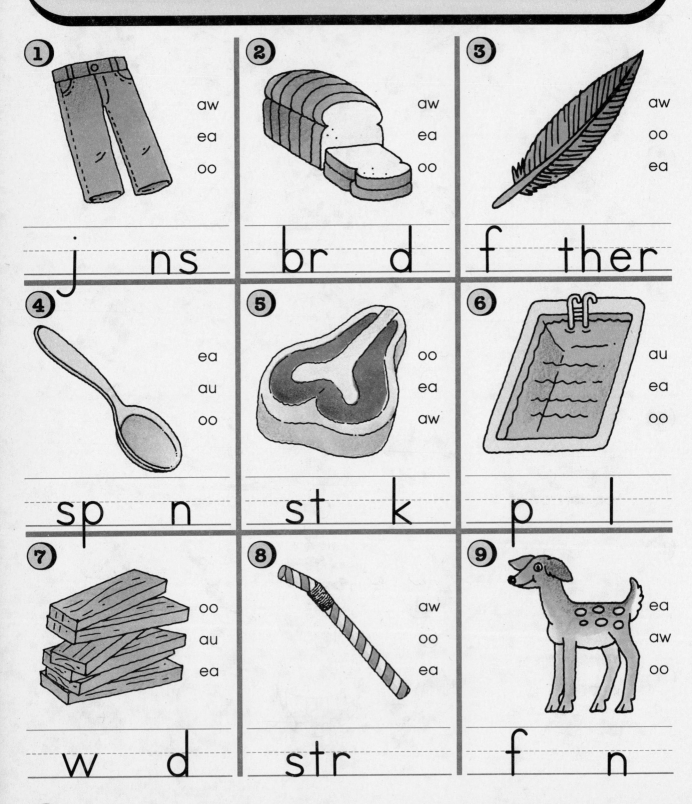

1. aw
   ea
   oo

   j __ ns

2. aw
   ea
   oo

   br __ d

3. aw
   oo
   ea

   f __ ther

4. ea
   au
   oo

   sp __ n

5. oo
   ea
   aw

   st __ k

6. au
   ea
   oo

   p __ l

7. oo
   au
   ea

   w __ d

8. aw
   oo
   ea

   str __

9. ea
   aw
   oo

   f __ n

Do it this way! The answer to each riddle rhymes with the picture. Find the answer in the box. Print it on the line.

toe	gray	pie	boat
spoon	bread	hook	saw

① It rhymes with <u>book</u>.
Hang a coat on it.
What is it?

_____

② It rhymes with <u>paw</u>.
You cut wood with it.
What is it?

_____

③ It rhymes with <u>doe</u>.
You have it on your foot.
What is it?

_____

④ It rhymes with <u>head</u>.
You can eat it.
What is it?

_____

⑤ It rhymes with <u>goat</u>.
You can row it.
What is it?

_____

⑥ It rhymes with <u>tie</u>.
Be sure to bake it.
What is it?

_____

⑦ It rhymes with <u>moon</u>.
You eat with it.
What is it?

_____

⑧ It rhymes with <u>hay</u>.
It names a color.
What is it?

_____

1. A baby deer is called a (seal, fawn, feather) .

2. A low seat is called a (stool, school, steam) .

3. A deep dish is called a (bean, book, bowl) .

4. A dish under a cup is called a (saucer, saw, stool) .

5. A crust filled with fruit is called a (pail, pea, pie) .

6. A sharp tool to cut wood is called a (seam, saw, say).

7. A person who makes meals is called a (cook, shop, whale) .

Now try this! Print the missing letters to finish the name of each picture.

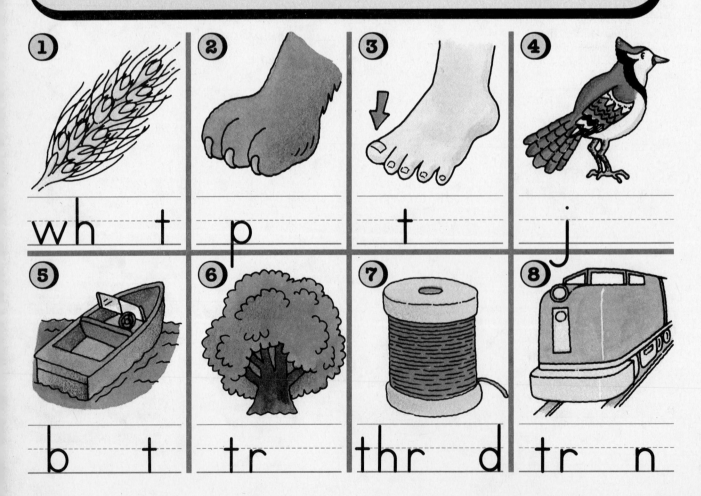

1. wh __

2. t __ p

3. t __

4. j __

5. b __ t

6. tr __

7. thr __ d

8. tr __ n

Here's what to do!

Here's what to do! Say the name of the picture. Find its name in the list. Print its letter on the line.

1
_____

2
_____

3
_____

4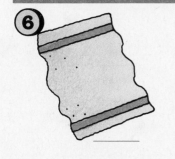
_____

a. clown	**j.** cow
b. cowboy	**k.** towel
c. mouse	**l.** flowers
d. shower	**m.** house
e. howl	**n.** town
f. owl	**o.** gown
g. now	**p.** pouch
h. crown	**q.** shout
i. cloud	**r.** mouth

5
_____

6
_____

7
_____

8
_____

9
_____

10
_____

Here's what to do! Say the name of each picture. Notice how it is spelled. Circle the **ou** or **ow** word in each sentence. Print it on the line.

owl   cow   cloud

1. I live on the edge of a small town.

2. My house is near a farm.

3. From my yard I can see cows and horses.

4. In summer, I watch the farmer plow his field.

5. At night, I can hear owls calling.

6. I like to watch the clouds around the hills.

7. Today I saw a flock of birds flying south.

8. They sense that winter is about to start.

Give this a try!

Find the answer to each riddle in the box. Print it on the line.

owl	cow	house	clown
flower	cloud	plow	ground

1 I am in the sky.
Sometimes I bring you rain.
What am I?

_____

2 I wear a funny suit.
I do many tricks.
I can make you smile.
What am I?

_____

3 I am in the garden.
I am very colorful.
Maybe I grow in your yard, too.
What am I?

_____

4 You can plant seeds in me.
The farmer must plow me.
What am I?

_____

5 I am wide awake in the dark.
I hoot and howl.
What am I?

_____

6 You can see me at the farm.
I eat green grass.
I give you good milk.
What am I?

_____

7 You can live in me.
I will keep you warm
and cozy.
What am I?

_____

8 The farmer uses me.
I help him make his garden.
What am I?

_____

Give this a try! Print an X beside each word in which **ow** stands for the long **o** sound.

crow   snow   clown   cow

(1) _____ how   (2) _____ snow   (3) _____ own   (4) _____ town

(5) _____ crowd   (6) _____ now   (7) _____ bowl   (8) _____ grow

(9) _____ low   (10) _____ plow   (11) _____ power   (12) _____ owl

(13) _____ slow   (14) _____ flow   (15) _____ know   (16) _____ show

(17) _____ brown   (18) _____ crow   (19) _____ crown   (20) _____ down

Now try this! Circle each **ow** word. Print an X in the correct column to show which sound it has.

	long vowel	diphthong
(1) We went to a good show last night.	_____	_____
(2) The star was a funny clown.	_____	_____
(3) We sat in the very first row.	_____	_____

Give this a try! Circle the name of each picture.

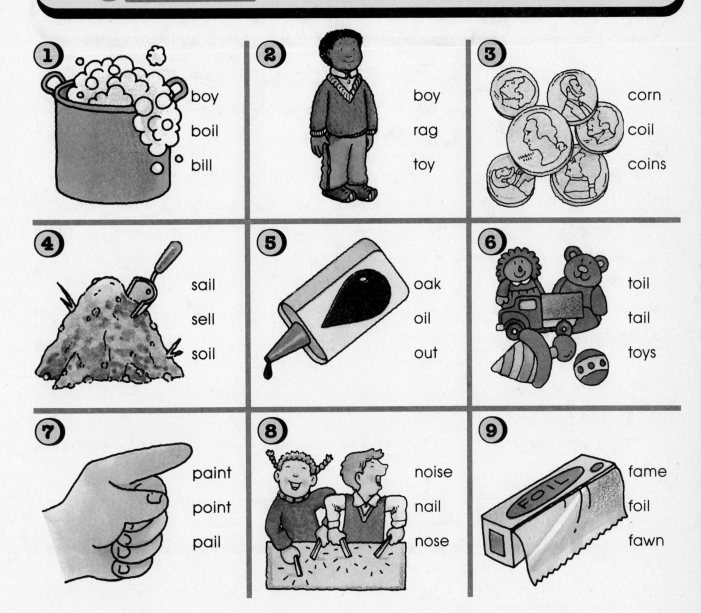

1. boy / boil / bill

2. boy / rag / toy

3. corn / coil / coins

4. sail / sell / soil

5. oak / oil / out

6. toil / tail / toys

7. paint / point / pail

8. noise / nail / nose

9. fame / foil / fawn

Now try this! Finish the sentences with a word from the box.

1. I have saved a few dollars and some _____ .

2. I will buy a _____ robot kit.

toy
coins

Here's what to do!

Read the story. Circle each **oi** word. Draw a box around each **oy** word.

The Runaway Toy

A boy named Roy had a birthday. His grandmother and grandfather gave him a choice of toys. Roy chose a toy train. He was a very happy boy.

Roy enjoyed his toy train, but it made too much noise. Roy took out a can of oil and oiled the toy. The oil made the train less noisy. It made it go faster, too.

One day Roy oiled it too much. The train went faster and faster. It raced around the room and out the door. Roy chased it out the door and down the path. The toy train rolled up to his sister, Joy.

"Look," said Joy. "This toy wants to join me outside."

"That's my toy train," said Roy. "It ran away from me. I used too much oil."

Joy gave the toy train to Roy.

"Thank you," said Roy. "From now on I will be more careful. I will not spoil my toy with too much oil."

Now do this!

Use the words you marked to answer the questions.

1 What was the boy's name? _____

2 What did he get for his birthday? _____

3 What made the train go fast? _____

4 What made Roy oil the train? _____

_____

_____

Do it this way! Find the word that will finish each sentence.
Print it on the line.

1 Floyd is a hungry _____ .

2 He does not want to play with his _____ .

3 Right now he would _____ a bowl of popcorn.

4 Floyd's sister _____ wants popcorn, too.

5 Joy _____ Floyd to make some.

6 Floyd pours some _____ in a pan.

7 The children listen for a popping _____ .

8 Did Floyd and Joy make a good _____ ?

Joy

oil

choice

joins

noise

boy

enjoy

toys

Give this a try! Circle **yes** or **no** to answer each question.

1 Is a penny a coin?   Yes   No

2 Is joy being very sad?   Yes   No

3 Can you play with a toy?   Yes   No

4 Is oil used in a car?   Yes   No

5 Is a point the same as paint?   Yes   No

6 Can you boil water?   Yes   No

7 Can you make a choice?   Yes   No

Now try this! Find the word that will finish each sentence.
Print it on the line.

___

1 _____ is glad the circus is in town.

2 She loves the _____ of the crowd.

3 She smiles and _____ at a funny clown.

4 She sees a _____ standing up on a horse.

5 Nothing can _____ the day for Joyce.

6 Joyce always _____ a day at the circus.

spoil
enjoys
Joyce
noise
points
boy

Here's what to do! Find the word that will finish each sentence. Print it on the line.

1. I bought a _____ pack of sugarless gum.

2. I _____ all five pieces into my mouth.

3. I _____ in a deep breath.

4. Then I _____ a giant bubble.

5. That great big bubble _____ .

6. I _____ I was in trouble.

7. The bubble broke, and pieces _____ everywhere.

8. Next time I _____ , I won't overdo.

| grew |
| blew |
| chew |
| flew |
| new |
| threw |
| knew |
| drew |

Now do this! Print the missing letters for a word that rhymes with each word.

1. few

st____

2. crew

thr____

3. grew

fl____

1. (Drew, Blew, Knew) wanted a pet.

2. He went to the (Crew, Dew, Flew) the Coop Pet Shop.

3. He saw puppies (chewing, stewing, mewing) on toy bones.

4. Baby birds (few, threw, grew) seeds around their cage.

5. What Drew really wanted was a (mew, stew, new) kitten.

6. He found a whole (chew, crew, grew) of kittens in the shop.

7. A (few, threw, grew) were very cute.

8. One kitten looked him in the eye and (flew, mewed, chewed) .

9. Drew (grew, dew, knew) that was the kitten he wanted.

---

1. Drew named him (Mews, Stews, Dews) because he always mewed.

2. That kitten (new, grew, chew) bigger every day.

3. Mews liked it when Drew (few, threw, mew) a toy to him.

4. He tried to hide under the (screws, grew, newspaper) .

5. From the window he watched birds as they (flew, crew, dew) .

6. When the wind (blew, drew, stew), Mews chased fallen leaves.

7. He licked drops of morning (mew, dew, chew) .

8. Before Drew (threw, few, knew) it, Mews was his best friend.

9. Drew really loved his (stew, new, flew) pet.

Give this a try! Circle the answer to each riddle.

1 You use it when you talk.

    spoil   joy   soil   voice

2 It means that something is wet.

    round   join   moist   oil

3 You see them do funny tricks.

    crowns   clowns   browns   clouds

4 You can live in it.

    house   mouse   plow   proud

5 It is something a dog can do.

    howl   coin   stew   new

6 Very hot water can do this.

    joy   boil   plow   oil

7 It is something to play with.

    owl   toy   crowd   how

8 It is something we can eat.

    mew   drew   stew   few

9 It means "not many."

    new   few   dew   stew

10 It means "dirt."

    soil   coil   boy   oil

11 The farmer uses it.

    frown   plow   down   cloud

12 A cat likes to chase it.

    house   shout   out   mouse

Now try this! Circle each **ow** word.

Chow Now?

"Moo – Moo," said Ms. Cow.

"How about some chow?

I want some now!"

"Not now, dear Ms. Cow.

Before you chow,

You help me plow!"

LESSON 87: Reviewing diphthongs

Do it this way! Finish each sentence with a word that rhymes with the word in the box. Print it on the line.

1 Girls and boys can shout with _____ .　　**toy**

2 A shout is one sound a _____ can make.　　**choice**

3 Animals' voices make different _____ .　　**pounds**

4 Lions can roar with a powerful _____ .　　**prowl**

5 A _____ makes a little squeak.　　**house**

6 Cows make a loud _____ when they moo.　　**poise**

7 These are just a _____ sounds of a voice.　　**dew**

8 _____ many others can you think of?　　**Now**

Now do this! Circle each **oi** or **oy** word.

Troy enjoys toys.

Troy enjoys noise.

So Troy likes toys

That make a loud noise.

176　**LESSON 87: Test: Diphthongs**

Here's what to do!
Add **re** to the word beside each sentence. Use the new words to finish the sentences.

When the prefix **re** is added, the word changes to mean **do again**.

rewind

The prefix is **re**.

The base word is **wind**.

He **rewinds** the tape.

replay

The prefix is **re**.

The base word is **play**.

Now he can **replay** the tape.

1. Every day I do things that I have to _____ . | **do** |

2. When I get up, I _____ my bed. | **make** |

3. I _____ my teeth after I eat. | **brush** |

4. I _____ my backpack before school. | **pack** |

5. When my camera needs film, I _____ it. | **load** |

6. I read and _____ my favorite books. | **read** |

7. I write and _____ my stories. | **write** |

8. Every night I _____ my alarm clock. | **wind** |

Here's what to do! Add **un** to the word beside each sentence. Use the new words to finish the sentences.

When the prefix **un** is added, the new word means the opposite of the original word.

Keys can **lock**.

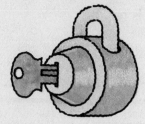

unlock

The prefix is **un**.

The base word is **lock**.

Keys can **unlock**.

① Every day we do things and _____ them. **do**

② We dress and _____ . **dress**

③ We tie our shoes and then _____ them. **tie**

④ We lock and _____ doors to go in and out. **lock**

⑤ We buckle our seat belts and _____ them. **buckle**

⑥ We pack our backpacks and later _____ them. **pack**

⑦ I am not _____ about all this undoing. **happy**

⑧ It just seems a little _____ to me. **usual**

Do it this way! Add **re** or **un** to the word beside each sentence. Use the new word to finish the sentence.

(1) Last night my baby sister _____ my backpack. `packed`

(2) She tried to _____ my homework with her crayon. `do`

(3) Now I have to _____ my story. `write`

(4) I am very _____ about it, too. `happy`

(5) My things are _____ around my sister. `safe`

Now do this! Print one word that means the same as each pair of words.

(1) not cooked _____

(2) spell again _____

(3) not safe _____

(4) use again _____

(5) not able _____

(6) play again _____

(7) not kind _____

(8) tell again _____

1 to <u>read</u> again

2 opposite of <u>lock</u>

3 to <u>fill</u> again

4 opposite of <u>tie</u>

5 opposite of <u>buckle</u>

6 to <u>heat</u> again

7 to <u>build</u> again

8 opposite of <u>pack</u>

9 to <u>write</u> again

_____

_____

_____

Give this a try! Add **dis** to each word. Use the new words to finish the sentences.

disorder
The prefix is **dis**.
The base word is **order**.

The toy chest is in **disorder**.

_____

1 My dog Wags _____ for a while.

appeared

_____

2 Then I _____ my shoe was missing.

covered

_____

3 "Why did you _____ me Wags?"

obey

_____

4 "You know I'm _____ when you take my things."

pleased

_____

5 "Wags, you are a _____ ."

grace

_____

6 Wags barked to _____ .

agree

7 He pulled my missing shoe from my

orderly

_____

_____

_____ toy chest.

1

Mr. Fixit will _____ the plug before fixing the telephone.

○ discolor
○ disconnect

2

The rider will _____ and let her horse rest.

○ dismount
○ distaste

3

Meg and Peg are twin sisters, but they _____ on many things.

○ disagree
○ disappear

4

The puppy _____ its owner and ran outside with her hat.

○ dishonest
○ disobeyed

5

Will loves green beans, but he _____ eggplant.

○ dislikes
○ disgrace

6

Kirk made the dirt appear, so he had to make it _____ .

○ disappear
○ distrust

_____

Here's what to do! Add **un, dis,** or **re** to each base word to make a new word. Print the new words on the lines.

un or dis		re or dis	
① _____ please	② _____ happy	① _____ honest	② _____ write
③ _____ obey	④ _____ easy	③ _____ add	④ _____ like

Now do this! Add **un, dis,** or **re** to each underlined word to change the meaning of the sentence. Print the new word on the line.

① Grandpa was <u>pleased</u> about the plans for his party.

_____

② He said he felt <u>easy</u> about getting gifts.

_____

③ Sadly Sue <u>wrapped</u> the present she had made.

_____

④ Then Jake said they would <u>obey</u> Grandpa just once.

_____

⑤ With a grin, Sue <u>wrapped</u> the gift.

_____

⑥ She <u>tied</u> the bow.

_____

⑦ Grandpa was not <u>happy</u> with his party after all.

_____

LESSON 91: Prefixes RE-, UN-, DIS-

Do it this way! Circle the prefix that makes sense in the sentence.

1. I stopped to _____ load my camera at the zoo.   dis   re
2. I _____ covered a large rhino looking at me.   re   dis
3. It seemed to be friendly, but I felt _____ easy.   un   dis
4. I know that may be _____ fair.   re   un
5. I don't mean to make the rhino _____ happy.   un   re
6. It's just that I _____ trust huge animals.   dis   un
7. It would be _____ honest to say it didn't scare me.   re   dis
8. A rhino could _____ able me quickly with its huge horn.   un   dis
9. I _____ agree with people who say a rhino is harmless.   dis   re
10. That huge beast looks really _____ safe to me.   re   un
11. I hope they remembered to _____ check the lock.   re   dis
12. I know I would _____ like a rhino away from its cage.   un   dis
13. I could tell it to be good, but it might _____ obey.   dis   re
14. I wish I had _____ read my books about rhinos.   re   dis

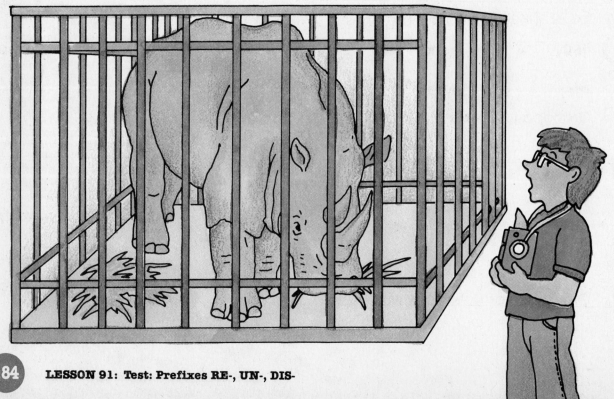

LESSON 91: Test: Prefixes RE-, UN-, DIS-

Do it this way! Print each word from the box beside a word that means the same thing.

Think about it!

① big _____

② happy _____

③ sick _____

④ small _____

⑤ quick _____

glad		fast
little	ill	large

Now do this! Circle the word in each row that means almost the same thing as the first word.

①	jolly	sad	big	happy	jump
②	junk	gems	trash	list	top
③	pile	heap	near	rest	stop
④	sleep	awake	nap	paint	read
⑤	sick	ill	quick	lazy	glad
⑥	quick	step	slow	pony	fast
⑦	sound	sad	noise	find	happy
⑧	large	huge	many	tiny	blue
⑨	close	move	let	shut	see

_____

_____

friend	gifts	noise	fast	kind
happy	races	easy	big	stops

Dear Pablo,

_____

I'm _____ that you came to my party.
(glad)

It was _____ of you to bring _____ .
(nice) (presents)

The _____ book looks _____ to read.
(large) (simple)

When I wind up the robot, it _____
(runs)

_____ and makes a funny _____ .
(quickly) (sound)

Thank you very much.

Your _____ ,
(pal)

Peggy

a. old	b. wet	c. start
d. full	e. slow	f. last
g. down	h. hot	i. good
j. short	k. out	l. well
m. few	n. winter	o. long
p. far	q. lower	r. shallow
s. shut	t. awake	u. thick

1 _____ dry   **2** _____ up   **3** _____ summer

4 _____ short   **5** _____ near   **6** _____ fast

7 _____ tall   **8** _____ bad   **9** _____ cold

10 _____ thin   **11** _____ sick   **12** _____ many

13 _____ stop   **14** _____ upper   **15** _____ first

16 _____ deep   **17** _____ new   **18** _____ empty

19 _____ open   **20** _____ in   **21** _____ asleep

Do it this way! Print the word in the box that means the opposite of each word.

open	full	ill	night	float
hot	strong		asleep	sit

1 awake

2 closed

3 empty

4 cold

5 healthy

6 stand

7 weak

8 sink

9 day

LESSON 93: Antonyms